sushi
taste and technique

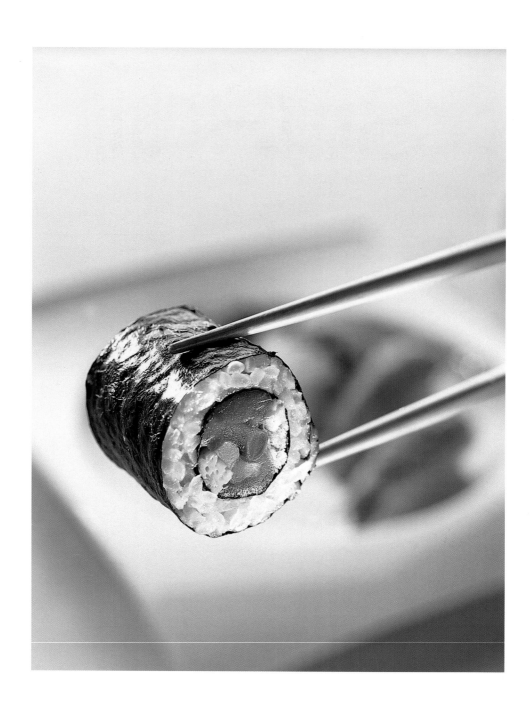

sushi
taste and technique

Kimiko Barber and Hiroki Takemura

Photography by Ian O'Leary

A DK Publishing Book

LONDON, NEW YORK, MUNICH,
MELBOURNE, AND DELHI

Project Editor Hugh Thompson
Project Art Editor Sara Robin
Book Editor Nasim Mawji
US Editor Julee Binder Shapiro
Designer Colin Goody
Managing Editor Gillian Roberts
Category Publisher Mary-Clare Jerram
Art Director Tracy Killick
DTP Designers Sonia Charbonnier, Louise Waller
Production Controller Louise Daly

First American Edition, 2002

02 03 04 05 10 9 8 7 6 5 4 3 2

Published in the United States by
DK Publishing, Inc.
375 Hudson Street
New York, NY 10014

Library of Congress Cataloging-in-Publication Data
Barber, Kimiko
Sushi taste and technique / Kimiko Barber and Hiroki
Takemura; photography by Ian O'Leary.
p. cm.
ISBN 0-7894-8916-3
1. Cookery (Fish) 2. Sushi   I. Takemura, Hiroki. II. Title.
TX747 .B327 2002
641.5952—dc21   2002023736

Color reproduction by GRB, Italy
Printed and bound in Italy by Graphicom

See our complete product line at
www.dk.com

Contents

What is sushi?
a history of sushi

The simple definition of sushi is "vinegared rice with a filling or topping of raw, cooked, or marinated fish, shellfish, vegetables, or egg." It is eaten as a snack, an appetizer, or as a main course and comes in many different forms, from bowls of rice scattered with fish and vegetables to rolled, pressed, and hand-formed sushi. Apart from its appeal as a delicious health food, sushi is exquisitely and often artistically presented.

In Japan, sushi is an everyday food. It began as a way of preserving fish and grew in popularity to become the nation's most famous food, not only in sushi bars, but also at home where it is prepared and eaten by the whole family. A Japanese ambassador once joked that sushi had done as much to raise the profile of Japan as the country's official efforts.

Sushi's arrival in Japan

No one knows exactly when sushi was invented, but fish was being pickled with rice in Southeast Asia as early as the 5th century BC. Some say that sushi came to Japan with the introduction of rice cultivation in the 4th century BC, while others believe that the practice was brought back by Buddhist priests returning from China after their training in the 7th century AD. The two Chinese characters for sushi, meaning "preserved

< Rice soon became a staple food of Japan after its introduction in the 4th century BC.

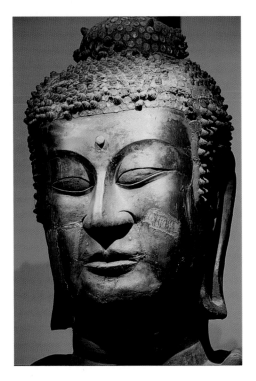

< Buddhist priests may have brought sushi back from China in the 7th century AD.

Changes in culinary culture

By the middle of the 15th century, rice was being boiled rather than steamed and lunch had been introduced. The Japanese were now eating three meals a day.

Then, at the beginning of the 17th century, the new government moved from the ancient imperial capital city of Kyoto to Edo [now Tokyo]. With the establishment of a powerful political and social structure came increased food production and more rice was grown. The increased rice production led to the wider use of other rice products such

fish" and "fish fermented in rice and salt," first appeared in Japan at the beginning of the 8th century AD.

Fish preserved in rice was sent to the land-bound capital of Kyoto as a form of tax payment. This early form of sushi, *nare zushi*, made from carp and rice packed into layers and fermented for up to a year, can still be found today. Something of an acquired taste, it is best described as a mixture of very mature Camembert cheese and Thai fish sauce.

∨ Meaning "sushi" in Japanese, this Chinese symbol first appeared in the 8th century AD.

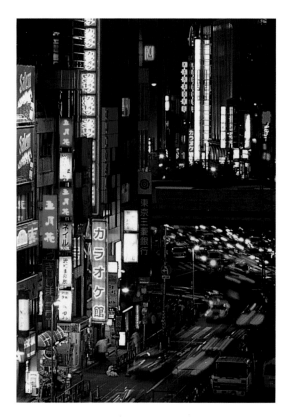

< The fast pace of life in Edo [now Tokyo] gave rise to the first fast food – *nigiri zushi*.

or hand-formed sushi, that we know today. He was the first chef to squeeze vinegared rice into a ball and top it with a slice of raw fish. Although the addition of rice vinegar had reduced preparation time, sushi chefs still made traditional pressed sushi, which took some time to make. The residents of Edo were notoriously impatient, so Yohei's newly invented *nigiri zushi*, which took only a few minutes to prepare, soon caught on.

World War Two further boosted the popularity of *nigiri zushi*. Food rationing prevented sushi shops from operating normally. When the Allied Occupation authorities issued a directive allowing the exchange of one cup of rice for 10 pieces of *nigiri zushi* and a sushi roll, they did not include any other type of sushi. To keep his shop open, the sushi chef was forced to make hand-formed sushi.

as rice vinegar. Instead of letting rice ferment naturally and produce lactic acid, rice vinegar was added to it, which reduced the time it took to prepare sushi from several days to just a few hours. However, sushi was still pressed in a box and the fish was marinated and boiled or grilled, not eaten raw.

Nigiri zushi – the first fast food

Yohei Hanaya, who set up a sushi stand in Edo in the early 1800s, is widely credited with being the inventor of the *nigiri zushi*,

Sushi stands disappear

It was at about this time that sushi stands began to disappear completely. Stores served mainly to-go customers during the day while stands were familiar

∧ Pressed sushi is the oldest form of sushi but almost disappeared after World War II.

Today it is winning recognition as the world's healthiest fast food. Although I am happy to see sushi gaining in popularity, I am filled with a mixture of delight and sadness when I see it in a supermarket – refrigerated and prepared by machines in factories, it is a far cry from what sushi is meant to be.

I am not dismissing to-go boxes or conveyer-belt sushi, but with fresh ingredients and a little care, you can make your own sushi at home and it will taste far better than anything you could buy ready-made.

features on Tokyo street corners in the evening. They were hauled into their alloted place and often strategically positioned to catch hungry men on their way back from public bathhouses. Customers shared communal bowls of pickled ginger and soy sauce and wiped their hands on a curtain hung behind them. A sure sign of a good sushi stand was a filthy curtain as this showed that more hungry diners had eaten there.

Sushi today

Sushi has come a long way since its origin as a means of preserving fish.

∨ A convenient snack, but store-bought sushi doesn't compare to homemade.

The sushi chef's training
mastering the art of sushi

I have often thought that if I could turn back time and start my life over again, I would like to train to be a master sushi chef. It probably wouldn't have been possible – apart from the fact that I am a woman and all sushi chefs are men, the arduous training can often take over 10 years to complete. This is my co-author chef Takemura's story.

Starting young

Chef Takemura left school at the age of 15 to work in a sushi bar in his local town of Matsuyama on Shikoku Island. He was lucky to get an apprenticeship in his hometown since many young aspiring sushi chefs have to leave home and work in faraway cities. He knew that many years of hard work lay ahead of him.

Menial tasks

His day started in the early hours of the morning when he would accompany the master or his senior chef to the local fish market as a bag carrier. Here, by carefully watching his master buying the fish for that day, he learned invaluable lessons about selecting only the freshest fish.

Once back in the store, his job was to clean it until it was spotless. His duties were to deliver platters of sushi around town, to collect dirty dishes, and to do the cleaning up. He was not allowed anywhere near the fish, let alone the counter where the sushi was prepared – that would take a few more years. He learned how to prepare sushi rice by quietly watching his master from a distance. When he was finally allowed to stand beside his master, it was to fan the steaming rice in order to cool it.

The counter

It was nearly 10 years before Takemura was finally allowed to stand at the counter at the front of the store. The counter is the most important part of every sushi bar, the stage where sushi chefs perform their art. By then he had moved on to a bigger sushi bar in Osaka, the second biggest city in Japan and the culinary capital. Here he quickly had to discard his regional accent so as not to offend the customers. Now an assistant,

or *wakiita*, which literally means "side cutting board," he was allowed to prepare fish for more senior chefs and to roll sushi for delivery. It took a few more years before he was finally allowed to stand at the counter as an *itamae*, which means "in front of the cutting board."

He was now a fully fledged sushi chef and could prepare his own sushi for customers, but his training did not end there. He had to contribute proactively to the success of the sushi bar, which meant that he had to cultivate his own loyal customers who would return regularly.

The master sushi chef

I first met Takemura in a top Japanese restaurant in London where he was head chef. We had a memorable meal that night, but it wasn't until we returned a few weeks later that I really understood what it takes to be a top sushi chef. Somehow he remembered us, what we ate and our likes and dislikes. He therefore adjusted the menu and the food he prepared for us accordingly.

I urge you to make your own sushi at home, but there is no better way to perfect your technique than to watch a master sushi chef at work.

Health benefits
sushi as a health food

Sushi is not only delicious, it's also very good for you. It is a wonderful bonus to be able to eat the food you love without paying the price for your indulgence. Great claims have been made for the health benefits of the typical Japanese diet of fish and rice. For example, average life expectancy for both women and men in Japan is one of the highest in the world.

Fish and seafood

Sushi is low in calories. White fish such as sea bass and red snapper have less than 100 calories per 3½ oz [100g]. Even richer fish such as mackerel, eel, and the fattier cut of tuna, *toro*, have less than 200 calories per 3½ oz [100g]. Oily fish

∨ Ginger root is pickled and served as a palate cleanser with sushi.

such as mackerel, sardine, and herring are high in omega-3 fatty acids, which can be effective in preventing heart disease, stroke, and arthritis.

Rice

More than half of the world's population lives on rice. An excellent source of carbohydrates and protein, it is gluten-free so suitable for those with wheat allergies.

Ginger

Like rice vinegar, ginger is an effective natural antiseptic. It aids digestion as well as boosting the immune system and helping the body to fight colds and flu.

Vinegar

Rice vinegar has amazing antibacterial properties, which have long been used to preserve food. It gently aids digestion

< Shredded nori adds a decorative touch to scattered sushi and soups.

Nori

Seaweed may be considered an unusual food by some, but it is highly nutritious. It contains protein, minerals – especially iodine – and is rich in vitamins A, B1, B2, B6, niacin, and C. It helps prevent cholesterol deposits from building up in the blood vessels. The darker the nori, the higher the quality.

Wasabi

Rich in vitamin C, wasabi stimulates the production of saliva and aids digestion. It has powerful antibacterial properties and is mildly antiseptic.

while also lowering the risk of high blood pressure and working as a mild pick-me-up. In its diluted form it also works as an effective skin conditioner.

Soy sauce

This is made from fermented soybeans, which are high in protein, magnesium, potassium, and iron. Soy products contain phytoestrogens, which have been successfully used to treat problems associated with menopause. A reduced sodium variety is now available. Tamari, which does not contain wheat, is a good alternative for those with wheat allergies.

> Soybeans are crushed with salt, wheat, and yeast and left to ferment to make soy sauce.

Basics

Utensils
dogū

Although you may have to hunt for the more obscure items, thanks to the ever-increasing popularity of sushi, most of the equipment you need to prepare it can be found in the housewares section of large department stores or in Japanese or Asian supermarkets. It's always preferable to have the right equipment, but in most cases you can improvise – a spring-form cake pan or a plastic box lined with plastic wrap are good substitutes for a pressed sushi mold, for example.

A set of good knives is a sound investment for any kitchen, but the only essential piece of equipment for which there is no substitute is a bamboo rolling mat for making rolled sushi. For those who enjoy cooking, adding to your collection of equipment can be a pleasure; most of the traditional equipment is inexpensive and has the advantage of having been designed specifically for sushi preparation.

< In most cases you don't need special equipment to make sushi.

> A sushi chef's knives are a treasured possession; he regularly cleans and sharpens them, and he wraps them up carefully when they're not in use.

Utensils
special equipment

These utensils will make sushi preparation easier and most are available from the housewares section in large department stores. It is always preferable to have the best tool for the job, but wherever possible, I have suggested good substitutes that can be found in any well-equipped kitchen. The only essential is a bamboo rolling mat for making rolled sushi.

V **Wooden rice tub** [hangiri]

Made of cypress wood and bound with copper wire, this broad low-sided tub is specially designed for preparing sushi rice. Its shape speeds the cooling process and makes it easier to fold in the vinegar mixture. The wood absorbs the excess moisture and helps give the rice its characteristic glossiness. The tub should be soaked in cold water and then wiped dry before use. After use, wash it in cold water and don't use dishwashing liquid. Dry it well to prevent it from becoming moldy, and store it upside-down in a cool dark place. A non-metallic salad bowl is a good alternative.

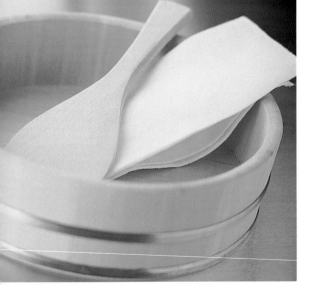

< **Cloth** [fukin]

Simple but very useful – a damp cotton or linen cloth is used to clean fish, utensils and to wipe the chef's hands.

< **Rice paddle** [shamoji]

A flat round-shaped paddle is traditionally used to serve rice and is made of bamboo or wood. Soak it in cold water before use to prevent rice from sticking to it.

> Bamboo strainer [zaru]

This traditional bamboo strainer is indispensable in the Japanese kitchen. It is used in many different cooking processes, from draining water from cooked foods to tenderizing fish skin and marinating mackerel. It must be dried thoroughly and air-dried well after use, or it will quickly turn musty and moldy. A plastic or metal colander does the same job, but a real bamboo strainer is inexpensive and more pleasing to handle.

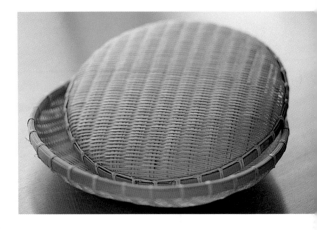

∨ Cooking chopsticks [sai bashi]

The chopsticks used for cooking are two or three times the length of ordinary chopsticks. They are long to protect your hands from the heat of cooking. Metal chopsticks are best for handling raw fish. Once you have mastered the technique, chopsticks become the most useful and versatile kitchen implements – an extension of your fingers, they enable you to manipulate food with just one hand. I can't cook without them.

You are more likely to injure yourself with a blunt knife, so take care of your knife and it will serve you well. Don't put it in the dishwasher, wash it by hand. Don't store it in a drawer with other kitchen tools that might chip the blade. If you have a knife block, slide the knife into a slot on its back, not on the sharp blade. If you cannot sharpen it yourself, have it done professionally; a good housewares store should offer the service.

Japanese knives are sharpened on one side of the blade, the cutting edge, which is always on the right side. A sushi chef normally has at least three different types of knife [pictured from left to right]:

Cleaver [deba bōchō]

This knife's heavy, curved blade is ideal for cutting through fish bones.

Vegetable knife [usuba bōchō]

In the hands of a sushi chef, this knife peels, cuts, and chops faster and finer than a food processor.

Fish knife [yanagi bōchō]

This long, slender blade is used for slicing fish fillets, cutting sushi rolls, and making decorative garnishes.

∧ Knives [hōchō]

A sushi chef's knife is as precious to him as a sword to a samurai warrior. The ancient craft of Japanese sword making is still practiced today, only it is used to forge kitchen knives made of superior quality carbon steel. These knives need to be properly cared for to maintain their hair-splitting sharpness. They should be sharpened by hand with a whetstone, never with a steel knife sharpener or grinding wheel.

> Shellfish tools

Shellfish and crustaceans such as crab and lobster are popular sushi ingredients, but often it is difficult to get to their meat. The specialized utensils below are not traditional sushi tools, but you'll find them indispensable.

Claw cracker

Crabs and lobsters have hard outer shells and some of their meat is found in their even harder claws. Although you can use a hammer or even the blade of a heavy kitchen knife to crack the shells open and get at the meat, it is easier to control the force – and also avoid unnecessary damage to the meat – if you use a claw cracker. If you don't have a claw cracker, a nut cracker is just as effective.

Crab pick

This is for reaching the more inaccessible meat in the recesses of the crab shell. A cocktail fork or a skewer is a good substitute, but the correct tool will make your work much easier.

Oyster knife

This is for opening oyster and scallop shells. You can use a screwdriver or the blade of small kitchen knife instead, but they are more likely to damage the oyster inside or worse still, cut your hands. To open an oyster, hold it steady with a dish towel wrapped around it, then insert the tip of the oyster knife blade and twist [see p122].

> Fish scaler

A fish scaler simply removes the scales
of the fish without damaging the flesh.
The back of a kitchen knife or even a
scallop shell make effective substitutes,
but again, having the right tool will
make the job much easier. When scaling
fish, a useful tip is to place it inside a
large plastic bag to catch flying scales.

< Japanese square omelette pan

The thick Japanese omelette [see p40–42]
is traditionally made in a square pan
with a depth of 1in [2cm]. This omelette
pan is usually made from thick, heat-
retaining metal and has a good solid feel
to it. It is possible to use a conventional
round skillet or frying pan of about 10in
[20cm] in diameter instead; simply trim
off the round edges of the finished
omelette to make it square.

< Bamboo rolling mat [makisu]
Essential for making any type of rolled sushi, the bamboo rolling mat is made of bamboo sticks woven together with cotton string. There is no real substitute for it, but the mats are not expensive and are easily available from any good housewares store. Choose a large tightly woven one. Wash and clean it with cold water and wipe dry immediately after use otherwise water will soak into the bamboo slats and attract mold.

> Pressed sushi mold [oshibako]
Traditionally made from cypress wood, which is the same wood usually used for the sushi counter, pressed sushi molds have removable bottoms and lids. They come in various sizes and may be square or rectangular in shape. To prevent the rice from sticking they need to be soaked in cold water before use and the excess water wiped away with a damp cloth. Care for a mold in the same way as a rice tub [see p18]. A rectangular spring-form pan or a plastic box lined with plastic wrap are good substitutes.

Ingredients
zairyō

Sushi's ever-increasing popularity has made it much easier to find the essentials in large supermarkets – staple ingredients such as Japanese-style short grain rice, nori seaweed, wasabi, rice vinegar, and Japanese soy sauce are readily available. Wherever possible, I have suggested substitutes, but for best results try to use the real thing. More unusual ingredients are available from specialty Japanese food stores or by mail order [see p250–51].

Ingredients such as dried gourd [*kampyo*] and shiitake mushrooms need to be reconstituted and flavored in a seasoned broth before use. You need to set aside time to do this, but they can be prepared in advance and kept in an airtight container in the refrigerator for up to three days. Most of the ingedients in the pages that follow have long shelf-lives if kept in the right conditions, so stock up and all you'll need to shop for when making sushi are the fish and vegetables.

< Sake, Japanese rice wine, is used to tenderize meat and fish and to enhance flavor; inexpensive cooking varieties are available.

> Fresh wasabi root is very difficult to find, even in Japan; it is normally sold in powdered form or ready-made in tubes.

Ingredients
pantry essentials

Many of the essential ingredients needed for making sushi at home –
Japanese-style rice, soy sauce, and wasabi, for example – are available
in large supermarkets these days. More specialty sushi ingredients
are easy to find in Japanese food stores and most have long shelf-lives.
I have suggested alternatives wherever possible.

> Japanese-style rice [kome]

Japanese short grain rice is essential for
sushi. It is high in starch, which gives it
its characteristic stickiness when cooked.
Store it in a cool, dark place in an
airtight container. Long grain rice such
as basmati is not suitable for sushi
since it is too hard and dry and is not
absorbent enough. The US, Spain, and
China grow short grain rice.

< Dried seaweed sheets [nori]

Sheets of nori are used for rolled sushi;
shredded, it makes an attractive garnish
for other types of sushi. It is made from
different types of Porphyra algae that are
washed and spread thinly to dry on mesh
sheets. Choose nori that is dark and
tightly grained; the thinner and greener,
the more inferior the quality. Store it in an
airtight bag or container in a dark place.

Japanese horseradish [wasabi]

This green horseradish is also known as *namida*, meaning tears, since it is fiercely pungent. A small amount is smeared in-between the fish and rice in hand-formed sushi. It should enhance the flavor of sushi, not overpower it. Buy it as a powder or as a paste in tubes.

∧ **Fresh wasabi roots**

The fresh root is native to Japan and grows there in clear mountain streams. It is expensive in its fresh form and is difficult to obtain outside of Japan.

∨ **Wasabi paste in tubes**

Although convenient to use, once opened, the wasabi quickly loses its pungency and flavor.

∧ **Powdered wasabi**

Widely available from supermarkets and Japanese stores, powdered wasabi has a long shelf-life and retains its flavor well. Make a stiff paste by mixing 1 tsp wasabi powder with 1 tsp water. Leave to stand for 5–10 minutes before using to allow the flavors to develop. The paste can be molded into decorative shapes and used as a garnish [see p51].

light soy sauce   dark soy sauce   tamari

∧ Soy sauce [shōyu]

This is probably the most important seasoning in Japanese cooking. Made from fermented soybeans, wheat, and salt, both light and dark varieties are available. Light sauce is saltier than the dark variety and not as thick. Dark soy sauce is used both as an ingredient and as a dipping sauce for sushi. Tamari is a wheat-free alternative that is more fragrant than soy sauce.

> Pickled ginger [gari]

Usually served on the corner of a sushi tray to accompany sushi, pink pickled ginger should be eaten a slice at a time. It cleanses the palate between mouthfuls and aids digestion. Although you can make your own, jarred ginger is normally of good quality. Once opened, it should be kept in the refrigerator.

> **Rice vinegar** [su]
Pale gold in color, Japanese rice vinegar has a mild, slightly tart flavor and leaves a subtle aftertaste. It is an essential ingredient in sushi, not just because it is used to flavor the rice. Rice vinegar is a preservative and also has antibacterial properties. It is available in Japanese food stores and supermarkets but cider or red wine vinegar diluted with a little water make adequate substitutes.

∧ **Japanese rice wine** [sake]
The national alcoholic drink of Japan, sake is one of the best accompaniments to sushi and can be drunk hot or cold. It is an important ingredient in cooking, where it is used to tenderize meat and fish, and to enhance flavor. Dry sherry is a good substitute. For cooking purposes, buy sake labeled as *ryori* sake, or inexpensive drinking sake.

> **Sweet rice wine** [mirin]
Also known as sweet sake, mirin is used strictly for cooking. If unavailable, use 1 tsp sugar for 1 tbsp mirin. Store in a cool, dark place after opening.

∨ Dried gourd [kampyō]

Kampyo is sold dried in long, thin strips. It is traditionally used as a filling for rolled sushi, chopped up as a topping for scattered sushi, and also makes a useful ribbon to tie parcels of stuffed sushi. It has a firm almost chewy texture. It is available from Japanese food stores. Before use, it needs to be reconstituted in a lightly seasoned broth [see right]. Prepared kampyo will keep refrigerated in a sealed container for three days.

∧ Preparing kampyo

Wash 1oz [30g] kampyo in cold water with a scrubbing action. Add 2 tbsp salt and rub in the water until soft [see above]. Rinse and soak in water for two hours or overnight [check packet instructions]. Drain, place in a saucepan with enough fresh water to cover, and simmer for 10–15 minutes. Add 16floz [500ml] dashi [see p39], 2 tbsp sugar, and 2 tbsp soy sauce, bring to a boil, then simmer for 10 minutes or until the kampyo is golden [see below]. Allow to cool in the stock before cutting to desired lengths.

∧ **Dried shiitake mushrooms**

These intensely flavored mushrooms are used as a filling in thick-roll sushi and as a versatile topping for scattered, pressed, and hand-formed sushi. They will keep for up to six months in a cool, dry place. They need to be reconstituted and seasoned before use [see right], but when soaked, good-quality shiitake are fleshy, plump, and meaty-tasting and stronger in flavor than fresh ones.

∧ **Seasoning shiitake mushrooms**

Soak 1oz [30g] dried shiitake mushrooms in 8fl oz [250ml] hot water for about 20 minutes. Drain, reserving the soaking liquid, and cut off and discard the stems. Add the mushrooms to 8fl oz [250ml] dashi [see p39] and the reserved liquid in a saucepan, and cook over a gentle heat for about 30 minutes or until the liquid has reduced by half. Add 1 tbsp mirin, then remove from heat and let cool in the liquid before using.

< **Perilla leaves** [shiso]

This aromatic Japanese herb belongs to the mint family. It resembles the stinging nettle, with its fringed leaves, but has no sting. It has a distinctive, pungent flavor and is often used as an edible garnish for sushi platters and sashimi arrangements.

∨ **Bonito flakes** [katsuo bushi]

The pink flakes are traditionally shaved from blocks of the dried, smoked, and cured bonito fish [see p58]. They are essential for flavoring dashi, the classic Japanese stock [see p39]. Packets of shaved bonito flakes are available from Japanese food stores.

∧ **Kelp** [konbu]

This seaweed grows near Hokkaido island, north Japan and is cooked, pickled, and then dried. Before use, wipe it with a damp cloth – do not wash it, because washing will destroy its flavor and nutrients. It keeps indefinitely in an airtight container. Choose dark – almost black – thick sheets, not thin, green, wrinkled ones.

< **Toasted sesame seeds** [iri goma]

Both black and white sesame seeds are available already toasted from Japanese food stores, but their nutty flavor tends to fade. To revive their flavor, dry-toast them in a pan over gentle heat for 1–2 minutes; keep them moving to prevent burning, which makes them bitter.

∧ Daikon radish

This large white radish is available from Asian supermarkets. Its subtle yet pungent flavor makes it an ideal accompaniment to sushi and sashimi. It can be cut into decorative shapes or shredded [see p48] and used as a garnish. It should be peeled and soaked in cold water before use.

∧ Making chile daikon relish

This mildly spicy fresh-tasting relish is the ideal accompaniment to Seared Beef Fillet and Red Onion Sushi [see p146]. Peel 8oz [250g] daikon, soak briefly, then grate it into a bowl. Deseed and finely chop a small red chile [or use a teaspoon of chile paste] and mix with the daikon.

< Lotus root [renkon]

The crunchy white root of the water lily, lotus root is white and honeycombed with holes. Highly seasonal, it is not always available fresh, even in Japan. Fresh lotus root is peeled and boiled in a mixture of water, sugar, and rice vinegar until soft. It is usually available canned or pickled in vinegar from Japanese stores, in which case it requires no cooking.

Basic recipes
kihon

Preparing sushi does not have to be time-consuming and complicated. Some of the ingredients may be new to you, but the basic recipes are straightforward and easy for any moderately confident cook to master. The key to quick and effortless sushi is good organization. If you prepare your ingredients beforehand, making sushi is simply a matter of assembly.

At the base of it all is the vinegared sushi rice, *sushi meshi*. Apprentice sushi chefs can spend several years just watching the master chef before being allowed to prepare the sushi rice, but here you'll find a simple step-by-step recipe that, with a little practice, will ensure success. Remember that you can make rice in the morning, store it at room temperature covered with a clean damp cloth and use it the same day.

Most cooks will be familiar with techniques such as making thin Japanese omelettes and scrambled eggs, but new recipes only require a little practice. Your first attempts at making sushi may lack the perfection of the master sushi chef's, but they will still look impressive enough and they will certainly taste delicious.

< Perfect sushi rice is firm, slightly sticky, and flavored with a delicate balance of sugar and vinegar, which gives it its characteristic gloss.

> Dried bonito flakes are added to the pot to make *dashi*, the basic Japanese stock.

Preparing sushi rice
s u s h i   m e s h i

Good sushi begins with good quality rice. Choose Japanese-style short grain rice, which is available from large supermarkets and Japanese food stores. The rice is first cooked, then it is flavored with a mixture of vinegar, sugar, and salt. The general rule is the stronger the filling or topping served with it, the more salty and less sweet the vinegar mixture. In Japan, every sushi bar has its own closely guarded vinegar mixture recipe. Once prepared, cover the rice with a clean damp cloth until needed; use it on the same day and don't refrigerate it. Soak the rice tub beforehand to prevent sticking.

Ingredients

1⅓ cups [10 oz/300g] Japanese short grain rice

11 fl oz [330ml] water

1 postcard size piece of kombu [optional]

for vinegar mixture:

4 tbsp Japanese rice vinegar

2 tbsp sugar

½ tsp salt

Preparation time
1 hour 30 minutes

1 Put the rice in a sieve and submerge in a large bowl of water. Wash it thoroughly and discard the milky water. Keep washing and changing the water until it is clear. Drain the water and leave the rice to stand in the sieve for 30 minutes.

2 If using kombu, make a few cuts in it to help release its flavor as it cooks.

3 Put the washed rice and water in a heavy-bottomed saucepan. Add the kombu, if using, and cover with a tight-fitting lid. Bring to boil over medium heat. Resist the temptation to lift the lid, and listen for the sound of boiling instead. When the water boils, turn the heat to high and cook for 5 minutes more.

4 Reduce the heat to low and simmer for 10 minutes, then remove from the heat and leave to stand for 10 minutes. Lift the lid and discard the kombu.

5 Heat the ingredients for the vinegar mixture in a non-aluminum saucepan, stirring until the sugar and salt have dissolved. Don't allow it to boil. Remove from the heat and set aside to cool. Transfer the cooked rice to a pre-soaked wooden rice tub or salad bowl. Pour a little of the vinegar mixture over a spatula into the rice.

6 Spread the rice evenly in the tub. Slowly add a little more of the vinegar mixture, using a slicing action to coat the grains of rice and separate them.

7 Fan the rice gently to cool it. Continue to fold the vinegar mixture into the rice with the spatula until it begins to look glossy and has cooled to room temperature.

Making Japanese stock
dashi

Dashi is the basic stock used to flavor many Japanese dishes. For a vegetarian version, omit the bonito flakes and double the quantity of kombu. If you prefer a stronger flavored stock, once strained, return the dashi to the heat and simmer gently for 10 more minutes.

Ingredients

1 postcard-size piece of kombu

4 cups [1 liter] water

a handful [⅓ oz/10g] bonito fish flakes

Preparation time
20 minutes

1 Prepare the kombu [see p37]. Put the water in a saucepan, add the kombu, and bring to a boil over medium heat. Just before boiling, remove the kombu and discard. Add the bonito flakes and bring back to a boil. Do not stir.

2 Remove from the heat when the dashi boils. When the bonito flakes have settled, strain the dashi through a cheesecloth-lined sieve.

Thick Japanese omelette
dashi maki tamago

Some sushi connoisseurs suggest that you begin your meal with a piece of hand-formed sushi topped with thick Japanese omelette in order to test a sushi bar's rice and vinegar mix. The omelette is slightly sweet in flavor and succulently moist. It's best to use a square Japanese omelette pan, but you can use a round skillet and trim the round ends off the omelette. Once prepared, it keeps for a day wrapped in plastic wrap and refrigerated.

Ingredients

6 eggs, beaten

4 fl oz [125ml] dashi stock [p39]

2 tbsp sugar

1 tsp salt

1 tbsp sake [optional]

1 tbsp mirin [optional]

1 tbsp vegetable oil for frying

Preparation time
20 minutes

1 Combine the eggs and all the remaining ingredients except the oil in a mixing bowl. Heat the oil in a square omlette pan; wipe away excess oil with a piece of folded paper towel.

2 Drop a small amount of egg mixture into the pan to test the temperature. If it sizzles, the pan is hot enough. Ladle a third of the mixture into the pan, so that the base is thinly covered.

3 Cook over medium heat until the surface begins to set and the edges begin to crisp.

4 Fold the omelette toward you in quarter sections using either chopsticks or a fork.

5 Push the folded omelette to the far end of the pan.

7 When the egg begins to set, fold it toward you in quarters with the first roll at the center.

8 Shape the omelette roll by gently pushing it against the side of the pan. Repeat the process until all the egg mixture is finished. Remove from the heat, and set aside to cool before cutting.

6 Add a little more oil to the exposed surface of the pan. Ladle in enough egg mixture to coat the base of the pan. Gently lift the folded omelette to allow the egg mixture to cover the entire base of the pan.

Scrambled eggs
tamago soboro

The key to preparing Japanese scrambled eggs is to use cooking chopsticks to stir them. This action gives them their stringy appearance and keeps the pieces separate. Try them as a colorful topping for scattered sushi.

Ingredients

2 eggs, beaten

1 tsp sugar

1 tsp salt

1 tsp vegetable oil

Preparation time
10 minutes

1 Combine the eggs, sugar, and salt in a mixing bowl. Heat the oil in a skillet over medium heat. Pour the egg mixture into the pan and cook, stirring constantly with chopsticks or a whisk.

2 When the egg begins to set, remove the pan from the heat but continue to stir for a fluffy consistency.

Thin Japanese omelette
usuyaki tamago

This thin omelette is folded and stuffed with sushi rice or thinly sliced, known as *kinshi tamago* or "golden shreds," and used as a topping for scattered sushi. This should make two to three omelettes, using an omelette pan about 7in [18cm] in size.

Ingredients

1 tsp cornstarch

1 egg

1 egg yolk

1 tsp salt

1 tbsp vegetable oil

Makes 2–3 omelettes

Preparation time
5 minutes per omelette

1 Dissolve the cornstarch in a tablespoon of water. Add to a mixing bowl with all the remaining ingredients except the oil and mix well. Heat the oil in a pan over medium heat [wipe away excess oil with a piece of folded paper towel], then pour in enough egg mixture to thinly coat the base of the pan.

2 When the omelette begins to set, pick it up and turn it over with a chopstick or fork to cook the other side. Don't allow the omelette to crisp or overcook – it should remain a golden yellow color.

3 Remove from the pan and transfer to an upside-down bamboo strainer or a plate lined with paper towel while you repeat the process to make more omelettes.

4 Either cut the round edges off the omelettes for omelette parcels or roll up and cut into fine shreds.

Seasoning deep-fried tofu
abura age

Deep-fried tofu, or *abura age*, can be eaten without any additional preparation but its flavor is greatly improved by this seasoning process. The pieces are cut in half and stuffed with sushi rice or chopped for scattered sushi. Deep-fried tofu is available seasoned or unseasoned at Japanese specialty stores. Seasoned tofu will keep for up to three days in an airtight container in the refrigerator.

Ingredients

3 pieces deep-fried tofu

½ quantity dashi stock [p39]

3 tbsp sugar

4–5 tbsp soy sauce

2 tbsp sake

2 tbsp mirin

Makes 6 pouches

Preparation time
30 minutes

1 Roll a chopstick over each piece of tofu to separate it. Cut each piece in half, then gently open it to make a pouch. Place in a bamboo strainer or colander and pour boiling water over both sides to remove oil.

2 Heat the remaining ingredients in a saucepan and add the tofu pouches. Simmer over low heat until most of the liquid has reduced, about 15–20 minutes. Remove from the heat and drain in a bamboo strainer or colander.

Making ground fish
soboro

This seasoned ground fish is often dyed pale pink with beet powder or vegetable dye. It makes a colorful filling for rolled sushi, brightens up scattered sushi, and can be a cheerful topping for children's pressed sushi. It is available in bottles from Japanese specialty stores, but is easy to prepare at home and will keep for up to four weeks in the freezer.

Ingredients

7oz [200g] white fish such as cod or flounder, skinned and bones removed

½ tsp beet powder or red food coloring

1 tbsp sugar

1 tbsp sake or water

½ tsp salt

Preparation time
45 minutes

1 Bring a saucepan of water to boil, add the fish, and boil for 10 minutes, then drain. Heat the fish in a saucepan over a low heat for about 5–10 minutes, stirring constantly to break it up. Don't let the fish burn.

2 Dissolve the beet powder or food coloring and sugar in the sake or water. Add it to the fish, stirring constantly to mix and fluff it up. Season with salt.

Garnishes and decorations
t s u m a / k a z a r i

It's not enough for sushi to simply taste delicious –
pay attention to presentation as well. Carrot, daikon,
and cucumber can be cut into flowers or shredded, and
handy knife work can transform a cucumber into a pine
branch to decorate sushi and soups. Wasabi leaves add
an artistic touch to sushi and sashimi arrangements.

Special equipment
flower-shaped vegetable cutter
Preparation time
about 5 minutes per decoration

making carrot flowers

1 Peel a small to medium-sized carrot and cut
into 1¾ in [4 cm] lengths. Place a piece of
carrot on its end on a stable cutting board and
use a vegetable cutter to cut it into flower-shaped
pieces. Repeat with the remaining pieces.

2 Slice the carrot pieces as thinly as possible
to make small flowers.

shredding cucumber

1 Take a 2½ in [6 cm] piece of cucumber and slice about ½ in [1 cm] off lengthwise for a flat edge. Cut several very thin slices, stopping when you reach the seeded core. Rotate the cucumber and do the same on the other side.

2 Place the slices on top of each other and slice thinly for a shredded effect. Soak in water for 10 minutes, then use as a garnish.

making an expert cucumber garnish

1 Insert a knife under the skin of a 4 in [10 cm] length of cucumber. Turn the cucumber against the knife to produce a long thin sheet.

2 Cut the cucumber sheet into several equal sized pieces, pile them on top of each other, and slice carefully into fine strands. Soak in water for 10 minutes, then use as a garnish.

making a cucumber pine branch

1 Cut a 2½ in [6cm] long piece of cucumber in half and cut off the skin on the sides. Make a series of lengthwise cuts about ⅛ in [2–3mm] apart, leaving a ½ in [1cm] base at the end.

2 Slice the piece of cucumber in half lengthwise.

3 Carefully fold in each of the cut strips of cucumber, tucking each one into the gap between itself and the next piece. Leave the last strip of cucumber unfolded.

making a wasabi leaf

1 To make 4 leaves, mix 8 tbsp wasabi powder to a smooth paste with a little water. Take a quarter of the mixture and work it into a cylindrical shape by rolling it in the palm of your hand.

2 Place the cylinder on a cutting board and pinch one end to make a stem. Flatten the cylinder with the flat part of a knife blade and mold into a leaf shape with your fingers. Smooth any cracks with a damp knife blade, if necessary.

3 Use a knife to score a stem and the veins of a leaf onto the wasabi. Repeat the process to make the remaining leaves.

Round and flat fish
sakana

The pages that follow will help you to identify fish that are suitable for sushi and sashimi and help you to buy them in their freshest state and in season – not only because their flavor and texture are better, but because they cost less. You will also learn which cuts of fish to choose and the correct way to prepare them.

I cannot stress enough the importance of buying the freshest fish possible for sushi and sashimi. A whole fish offers more clues to its freshness than a small cut piece, and although it is not always practical to buy a whole fish, it is often possible to see it before it is filleted. Check the following when buying fish:

• The eyes – should be clear, bright, and plump, not cloudy and sunken.

• The gills – should be a bright pink or red, not a dark, murky red.

• The body – press it gently; it should feel firm and springy, not spongy and sticky.

• The smell – fresh fish smells clean and fresh from the sea, not unpleasantly fishy.

You will become more confident in your judgment with a little experience. Make friends with your fishseller – he or she should be happy to answer your questions.

< Fresh fish fillets should be moist but not watery, almost translucent, and firm enough to slice easily with a sharp knife.

> Whole specimens often give a better idea of the freshness of the fish. High quality fish should look like it has just come out of the sea.

Horse mackerel
aji

For the Japanese, horse mackerel are one of the most popular *hikari mono*, or "shiny things," a term that refers to oily fish with shiny silver/blue skin. It is inexpensive, available throughout the year, and has a simple yet satisfying taste. However, outside Japan, its bony skeleton, sharp spines, and strong flavor make it something of an acquired taste – it is often discarded when caught on mackerel lines. Like all oily fish, horse mackerel can lower blood cholesterol levels, which can help prevent heart disease and strokes.

The sharp, bony plates on the side of the horse mackerel's tail must be removed before eating.

Availability
There are 13 varieties of horse mackerel widely distributed in shallow waters around the world. Although available year-round, horse mackerel are at their best at certain times of the year: in Australia and Japan they are best in winter; in North America, along the east coast, they're at their prime in spring and summer, and in Europe they're best in summer and fall.

fillets are usually sold with the skin left on

Horse mackerel fillets

As for all oily fish used in sushi, horse mackerel are served with the skin intact. They are milder in flavor than mackerel.

distinctive firm, red flesh

The horse mackerel has a bluish silver body with a slightly darker back.

Herring and sardines
nishin / iwashi

Herring and sardines are closely related; there are some 180 varieties found around the world. Both of these distinctively flavored fish are classified as *hikari mono*, or "shiny things" by the Japanese. Herring and sardines are rich in beneficial oils and have recently been recognized as very healthy. However, like *aji*, they are rarely seen on sushi menus, mainly because they spoil very quickly once caught. In Japan, herring are highly valued for their roes, which are known as *kazunoko*, or "yellow diamonds."

Herring and sardine fillets
Herring and sardines need to have their scales removed, but the fillets are served with the skin intact.

scales are easily removed

sardine fillets can still contain lots of feathery bones

Availability

Sardines are commercially important in North America and are available year-round, but are not at their best during summer. Herring are available year-round in Europe, but are best from May to September. They are in season between December and February on the Pacific coast of North America, when they produce herring roe, and between winter and spring on the Atlantic coast.

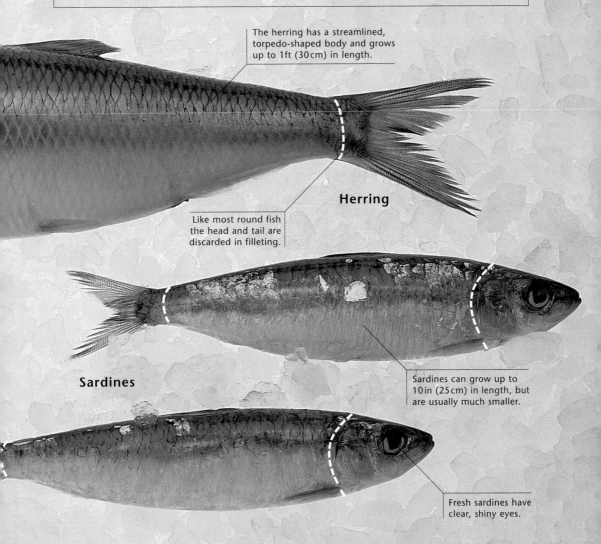

The herring has a streamlined, torpedo-shaped body and grows up to 1ft (30cm) in length.

Herring

Like most round fish the head and tail are discarded in filleting.

Sardines

Sardines can grow up to 10in (25cm) in length, but are usually much smaller.

Fresh sardines have clear, shiny eyes.

Bonito
katsuo

Sometimes confused with the skipjack tuna, bonito is related to
tuna but actually belongs to the mackerel family. Traditionally, it
is fished with a single rod rather than a large trawling net, which
might damage its flesh, and is one of the fastest swimmers in the
sea. Bonito features in nearly every aspect of Japanese cuisine. It is
eaten in sushi and marinated or lightly grilled as sashimi. Dried
and shaved, it is used to make dashi, the basic Japanese stock.
Bonito is often served with grated ginger, which complements
its distinctive full, rich flavor.

Each fillet gives two large
blocks which are then cut
into smaller pieces.

The bonito's back is
dark-green or blue
with dark stripes.

Bonito have
tails with a
reddish tinge.

Availability

A medium-sized migratory
fish, bonito are prevalent in
the warm waters of the
Pacific. They migrate
northward along the
Japanese coast, starting in
February and appear on the
menu of Tokyo sushi bars in
early May, signaling the
beginning of summer. They
come into season in North
America in spring to summer;
outside Japan, the rest of the
world relies on this supply.

Bonito fillets
For sushi and sashimi, the skin is left on. Bonito is lightly grilled, then submerged in cold water.

rosy colored flesh

Cuts from the back are more meaty than from the belly [see above].

Unlike the skipjack tuna the bonito has no dark stripes on its belly.

Bluefin tuna
maguro

Although related to the mackerel, a fully grown bluefin tuna can weigh up to 600lb [250kg]. The Japanese classify tuna as a red meat fish and divide each huge fillet into two blocks – upper and belly. These are then graded and priced according to their fat content – the fattiest part of the fish, the belly, being the most prized and the most expensive. Even in busy sushi bars in Japan, tuna is bought by different cuts: the pale, fatty belly part, the oily back fillet, and the lean, dark tail end. Tuna has a soft texture and a clean taste.

Availability

Other varieties of tuna include *mebachi* [big-eye tuna], *binnaga* [albacore], and *kiwada* [yellowfin tuna]. Tuna are available all year in sushi bars worldwide, but are best from fall to winter in Japan, Australia, and Europe, while summer is the best season in North America. Tuna has become a classic ingredient in hand-formed sushi [see p208–17] and rolled sushi [see p184–207].

Tuna steaks are usually cut from the back or tail.

The meat around the spine, *akami,* is very low in fat and dark red in color; it is the least valued by the Japanese.

Tuna steaks

Avoid tuna that has become discolored, gray, or is leaking moisture, since this is an indication that it is not fresh. Ask your fishseller to cut a fresh steak for you rather than buying a pre-cut piece.

distinctive red meat from the tail [see below]

Chu toro comes mainly from the upper part of the tuna and has a very full and rich flavor.

The most prized cut of tuna comes from the belly; *oho toro* is light pink, marbled with fat, and melts in the mouth.

Mackerel
saba

One of the tastiest oily fish available, mackerel must be put on ice as soon as it is caught, otherwise its flavor is lost; Japanese fishermen go to great lengths to protect its freshness and quality. Before modern transportation, the land-bound former capital city, Kyoto, was too far inland to enjoy fresh mackerel, so pressed sushi, or *battera*, was invented as a method of preserving it. This type of pressed sushi is still popular in the region to this day. For hand-formed sushi, mackerel is first salted and marinated in a vinegar mixture [see p92–3]. It is often served with grated ginger, which balances its strong flavor.

Look for clear eyes with no traces of blood in them.

Less fresh mackerel develop a yellowish tinge in this region.

Its silvery white belly should be plump and firm to the touch.

Mackerel fillets
Intensely flavored, mackerel is high in protein and rich in beneficial oils.

thin, parchment-like skin must be removed [see p93] since it can harbor bacteria

Mackerel has a shiny, blue-green back with distinctive dark tabby markings.

Availability
There are three varieties of mackerel widely distributed all over the world: Pacific mackerel, Atlantic mackerel, and spotted mackerel, which are found in Australia, New Zealand, and the Hawaiian Islands. Available throughout the year, mackerel are in season from February to June in Europe, from summer to fall in North America, and in the winter in Australia and New Zealand.

Salmon
sake

With its bright orange flesh, salmon is probably the most easily recognizable fish in sushi bars outside Japan. However, in Japan it is almost never eaten raw, but usually grilled or salted. There are two types of salmon, the Atlantic and the Pacific – of which there are six varieties. Wild salmon grow to maturity in the open sea, feeding on the fish and crustaceans that give the flesh its distinctive color. Commercially farmed salmon, although noticeably inferior in taste and texture to wild salmon, is a far less expensive option and the quality is gradually improving. Look for "tagged" salmon, which comes from farms where the fish are raised in better conditions.

The fillet is cut from the side of the whole fish.

Wild salmon have ragged tails.

Availability

Both Pacific and Atlantic salmon are widely farmed, resulting in inexpensive salmon that is available year-round. However, the pollution from intensive salmon farming threatens wild fish stocks already reduced by overfishing. Wild salmon are in season in spring in Australia, from February to August in Europe, and from summer to fall in North America.

the fattier part
of the steak

Steaks and fillets

These are readily available at most
fish counters. Fillets may be more
expensive but they are a better
shape for sushi [see p88].

firm, pink meat
with no gaps

When in season,
salmon have fat,
plump bellies.

Steaks are cut
from the middle
of the fish.

The inside of the gill
should be bright red;
avoid salmon with
very dark red gills.

John dory
matō dai

This fish has a distinctive spot behind its gills, which gives it its other name – St. Peter's fish. The spot is said to denote the place where St. Peter put his thumb when picking it up. John dory are rarely found in Japanese waters so are less common on Japanese sushi bar menus, but their firm, delicate-tasting white meat makes them suitable for any type of sushi and a very popular sushi ingredient in Australia.

John dory fillets
John dory has a heavy bone, which makes it easier to fillet; it is not very fleshy.

relatively small and expensive fillets

Availability

John dory lives in the East China Sea, the Atlantic, and also in the waters near Australia and New Zealand. It is available most of the year in Europe, but is not as good between June and August. It comes into season in Australia and New Zealand during the winter months.

John dory has smooth skin with no scales.

The gray spot has earned it the name "target dory."

Sea bass
suzuki

The Japanese regard the white flesh of the sea bass nearly as highly as
they do *tai* [red snapper] and associate the fish with success in life –
another name for it is *shusse uo*, meaning "advancement in life" or
"promotion" fish. This is because, as it grows, the sea bass develops
through a series of stages, starting off in fresh water and ending up in
the sea. It is known by a different name at each stage and only when
the sea bass has lived in the sea and grown to a particular size does
it earn the name *suzuki*. The fish has firm white meat with a delicate
flavor and is a good topping for hand-formed sushi.
Cut paper thin, it makes elegant sashimi.

Look for clear
unsunken eyes.

Sea bass scales are
tough and need to
be removed before
filleting [see p72].

Sea bass fillets

Usually, sea bass fillets are thick and meaty – ideal for sushi.

fillets sold with skin on

pale, almost transparent flesh, with typical pink undertones

Spines and fins are usually intact on wild sea bass.

Availability

Wild sea bass are in season in early summer in Japan, year-round in North America, in late summer in Australia, and in winter in Europe. Farmed bass are widely available and reasonably priced. However, flavor and texture bear little comparison to those of the wild fish. Sea bass should not be confused with the Patagonian Toothfish, a very endangered species, often sold as Chilean sea bass.

Red snapper
tai

Wild red snapper have unbroken, spiny fins.

The Japanese consider *tai* to be the best and most noble fish in the sea and the "true" *tai* (*ma dai*), from the Seto Inland Sea, to be the finest of all. Its firm pink and white, broad-flaked flesh is delicately flavored. A whole handsome grilled *tai* with its tail pointing up on the New Year's Day celebration table is as important as a roast turkey at Thanksgiving or Christmas in the West. Its demand far exceeds its supply, so it's no wonder that the name *tai* has been added to many non-related species. Real *tai* is only available in Japan, but red snapper, sea bream, and porgy, which are often translated as *tai*, are close substitutes.

Availability

Ma dai are best in spring in Japan, while the North American substitute, porgy, come into season between September and May. In Europe, red snapper and sea bream are available between June and December; in Australia and New Zealand, red snapper, better known as broadbill snapper, or just plain "snapper," are best during fall.

skin is often
left on for
sushi [p94]

Red snapper fillets
Its delicately flavored pink
and white flesh make red
snapper a popular
ingredient in sushi.

characteristic
pink and
white flesh

Look for clear,
shiny eyes.

The red snapper's thick scales
need to be removed before
filleting [see p72–75].

Filleting round fish
for sushi

It is more economical to buy a whole fish and also easier to assess the freshness whole. Known as *sanmai oroshi*, or "three-piece filleting" by the Japanese, the end result is two fillets and the skeleton. Use a sharp knife, and work within easy access of running water.

Special equipment

fish scaler

large plastic bag

pair of small tweezers or pliers

Preparation time
about 15 minutes

1 Scale the fish by holding the head and firmly drawing the scaler from the tail to the head. Hold the fish under cold running water or place inside a large plastic bag to catch the flying scales.

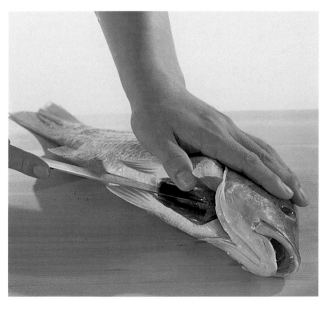

2 Insert the tip of a sharp knife into the belly and cut open the underside of the fish from the gills to the fin near the tail. Be careful not to damage any internal organs.

3 Cut from the tail fin to the tail. Open the slit and remove the innards by pulling them firmly toward the tail. Discard the innards, and wash the cavity and the knife.

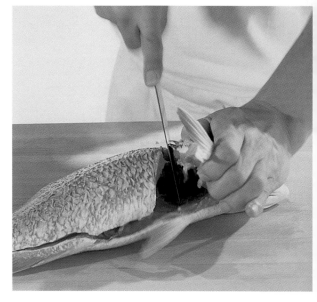

4 With the head facing you, carefully insert the knife into the back of the fish at the tail. Cut along toward the head with the knife blade resting on the backbone.

5 Hold the fish by its gills on one side and cut through the body to the spine. Turn the fish over and cut through the other side. Finally, cut through the spine to remove the head.

6 At the tail, insert the knife through the slit made on its back to the slit made in its underside so that the blade passes just over the skeleton. Keeping the blade flat and working away from the tail, cut the fillet loose with a firm sawing action. Use the ribs and backbone to guide the blade. Finally, slice through the skin that attaches the fillet at the tail.

7 Turn the fish over and repeat steps 4 and 6, then cut away the second fillet.

8 You should have two large equally sized and shaped fillets and the skeleton.

9 With the knife almost horizontal, carefully cut the stomach cavity lining and any rib bones away. Run your hands lightly over the surface of the fillets to feel for any pin bones and remove with tweezers or small pliers. Trim the edges of the fillets.

10 To skin the fillets, rub some salt on your fingers to provide a better grip. Grasp the tail and cut at a shallow angle as far as the skin, being careful not to cut through it.

11 Keeping the blade still and almost parallel to the cutting board, pull carefully on the fish skin, working it from side to side so that the skin comes away.

Turbot
hirame

There is no direct translation for turbot, but the Japanese classify all flat fish with eyes on the left of the head as *hirame*. Similar looking but smaller fish from the Indian Ocean, the South China Sea, and off the coast of Queensland, Australia are often exported to Japan as *hirame*. Of all *hirame*, the white flesh of the turbot is considered to have the most exquisite flavor and a meaty, succulent texture. It is excellent eaten raw in sushi and as sashimi.

Fresh fish do not have sunken eyes.

Turbot have a natural camouflage; color can vary from gray-brown to dark chocolate brown.

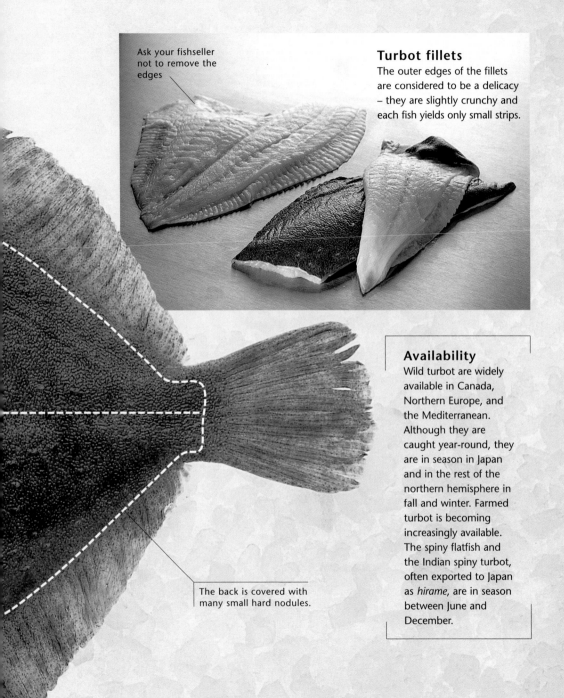

Ask your fishseller not to remove the edges

Turbot fillets

The outer edges of the fillets are considered to be a delicacy – they are slightly crunchy and each fish yields only small strips.

The back is covered with many small hard nodules.

Availability

Wild turbot are widely available in Canada, Northern Europe, and the Mediterranean. Although they are caught year-round, they are in season in Japan and in the rest of the northern hemisphere in fall and winter. Farmed turbot is becoming increasingly available. The spiny flatfish and the Indian spiny turbot, often exported to Japan as *hirame*, are in season between June and December.

Brill
hirame

Another member of the *hirame* family [fish with eyes on the left side of the head], brill is slightly smaller than turbot [see p76–7] and is a popular ingredient in sushi. It should not be confused with megrim, which is similar in appearance but has a slightly watery, bland flavor and is the least popular of the *hirame*. If in doubt in a sushi bar, ask the sushi chef what the fish is called in English since it will probably be served under the blanket Japanese term of *hirame*.

A fresh brill has a full, plump head.

Brill fillets
If buying a fillet of brill, insist on a back fillet – it has more meat.

firm, meaty flesh with a yellow tinge

Skin is olive to brown and should not feel slimy.

Availability
The name brill is given to several different types of flat fish around the world, but they are all very similar and can be used for sushi in the same way. In Europe, brill comes into season from June to February, but like most flat fish, it is at its tastiest during the fall and winter months. The North American brill is in season year-round. Brill is also comercially fished in New Zealand and Australia.

Lemon sole
karei

Despite its name, lemon sole is no relation to Dover sole and is in fact a type of flounder. The Japanese regard it as one of the *karei* family: flat fish with eyes on the right side of the head. Among the *karei* group, lemon sole is often overshadowed by the other more highly prized flat fish such as halibut, flounder, and plaice. However, its succulent white flesh makes it suitable for all types of sushi and sashimi.

Lemon sole fillets
With a delicate almost sweet flavor and succulent texture, lemon sole is a popular sushi ingredient outside Japan.

thicker back fillets are better for sushi and sashimi

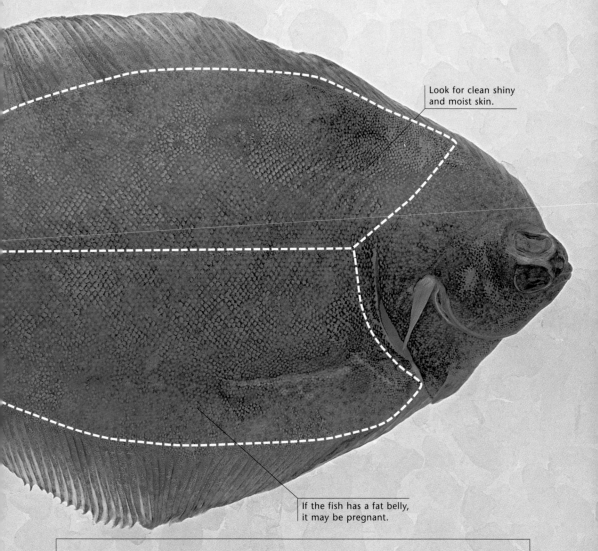

Look for clean shiny
and moist skin.

If the fish has a fat belly,
it may be pregnant.

Availability

Lemon sole are widely
available in the North
Atlantic, the North Sea,
and the Norwegian Sea.

In Europe, they are caught
throughout the year, but are
at their best between May
and March. They are
available year-round in

North America, but should
be avoided from April to
September since this is when
they breed and the flesh
tends to be less flavorsome.

Halibut
ohyō garei

A member of the *karei* family [flat fish with eyes on the right of
the head], halibut is the largest of the flat fish and often measures
up to 6½ft [2m], and can grow to as long as 13ft [4m]. It has large,
powerful jaws and is known for putting up a good fight when
caught in the fishermen's net. To really appreciate its dense, meaty
flesh, which has an excellent flavor, it is best to choose younger,
smaller fish, sometimes called chicken halibut; the bigger the
fish, the drier and blander it tends to be.

Availability
Halibut are plentiful both in the
Atlantic and in the Pacific. They
come into season in the US
between May and September
and between June and March
in Europe. Like other flat fish
from the northern hemisphere,
they become oilier and more
succulent during the winter.

bone is removed
before being sliced
for sushi [see p90–91]

Halibut steak
Because of the size of the
fish, halibut is often sold in
steak form outside of Japan.

It has sharp, inward
curving teeth and is
the thickest-bodied
of the flat fish.

The halibut has gray to
olive-gray skin with a
pearly white underside.

Filleting flat fish
for sushi

Japanese sushi chefs traditionally fillet flat fish using the "five-piece filleting" method, so-called because the end result is four equally sized fillets and the skeleton. Although flat fish don't have scales like round fish do, they are nearly always skinned for sushi.

Special equipment

pair of small tweezers or pliers

Preparation time

About 15 minutes

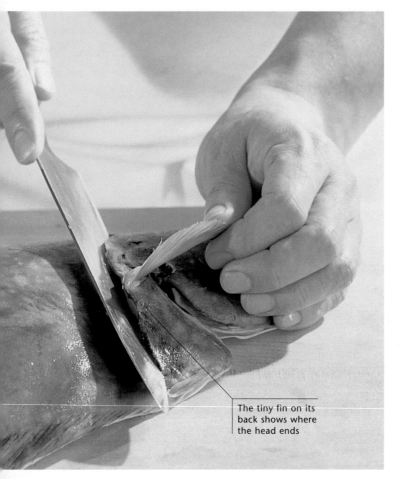

The tiny fin on its back shows where the head ends

1 Insert the blade at a 45° angle just behind the central fin, and cut off the head. The innards should come away as you pull off the head.

2 Place the fish on its lighter colored belly and cut around one side of the fish just inside the outer fin.

3 Rotate the fish and carefully cut around the other side.

4 Starting at the tail, cut into the fish as far as the backbone. Cut down the middle of the fish, working toward the front.

6 Turn the fish around and do the same to the fillet on the other side, this time starting at the tail end.

5 Turn the fish around so the tail is facing you. With the knife at a slight angle, ease the blade into the central cut, feeling for when it reaches the bones. Using the bones to guide the knife, work down the length of the fish, cutting the fillet away from the skeleton. Long smooth strokes will give a cleaner, less jagged cut.

7 Flat fish are nearly symmetrical, so simply turn the fish over and repeat steps 4 to 6 to cut the fillets from the other side of the fish.

8 Cutting at an angle, carefully remove the stomach cavity lining and pull out any little bones with small tweezers or pliers. Trim the fillets to an even shape.

9 You are left with four equally sized fillets. To skin them, see p75, steps 10 and 11.

Slicing fish fillets
for sushi

Depending on the type of sushi, fish fillets can be sliced in four different ways. For hand-formed sushi, the fillet is cut diagonally into thin slices; for hand-rolled and thick-roll sushi, it is then cut into ½ in [1cm] square sticks. Pressed sushi works best with large, flat pieces of fish, and scattered sushi requires uniform-size strips. Choose a skinless fish fillet that is roughly hand-sized and as even a shape as you can find.

Ingredients

10oz [300g] skinless fish fillet about 1–2in [2.5–4cm] thick

Preparation time
About 15 minutes

For Hand-formed Sushi [see p208–17], cut diagonal slices about ¼ in [5mm] thick. Hold the knife at a 45° angle to the fish. Resting your fingertips lightly on the fish, gently work the knife through the fish to produce even slices. The first slice may not be suitable for hand-formed sushi, but it can be used for thin-roll sushi.

For Pressed Sushi [see p168–83], cut large, flat pieces of fish. Resting one hand lightly on the fillet and keeping the blade parallel to it, carefully cut a slice as thin as you can – about ⅛ in [3mm] thick – from the top of the fillet. Repeat as needed.

For Hand-rolled Sushi and Thick Roll Sushi [see p192–5 and p204–7], slice the fillet as for hand-formed sushi [see left] but cut the pieces slightly thicker. Next slice the pieces lengthwise into ½ in [1cm] square sticks. For hand-rolled sushi, each stick should be about 2¾ in [6cm] long.

For Scattered Sushi [see p132–9] or Sashimi [see p240–3], cut slices ½ in [1cm] thick – these can also be cut into strips for rolled sushi.

Slicing fish steaks
for sushi

Many large fish are often sold as steaks and need some preparation before they can be sliced for sushi. Once the bones and skin have been removed and the fish shaped into blocks, it can be sliced for scattered, rolled, and hand-formed sushi and sashimi.

Ingredients

1 fish steak about 8oz [250g] from any large fish such as salmon or halibut

Preparation time
About 15 minutes

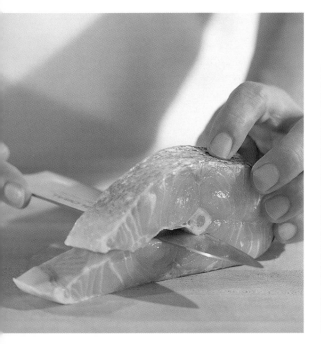

1 Place the steak on the cutting board skin-side-down. Hold it securely in position and cut the steak in half, working a sharp knife carefully under the central bone.

2 Position the half of the steak with the bone skin-side-down. Holding it steady, repeat step 1 and carefully cut out the bone.

3 Remove any bones that might still be in the flesh [see p93] and, using a sharp knife, trim any fatty tissue from the fillet.

4 Position the fish with the skin-side down. Holding the blade parallel to the cutting board, carefully cut off the skin.

5 Cut the resulting evenly shaped pieces of fish into ½ in [1cm] strips for scattered sushi, hand-formed sushi, or sashimi.

6 Alternatively, cut the slices in half lengthways into pencil-thin strips, and use for rolled sushi.

Marinating mackerel
shime saba

Mackerel is inexpensive, available year-round and yet it is not as popular as it should be. Only the freshest mackerel is eaten raw because it deteriorates rapidly if not handled properly once caught. Marinating mackerel in vinegar enhances the flavor and also helps to preserve and tighten its oily flesh, making it easier to slice. It can be prepared up to six hours in advance.

Ingredients

4 mackerel fillets,
about 5oz [150g] each

about 8 tbsp sea salt

16fl oz [500ml] rice vinegar

2 tbsp mirin or
3 tbsp granulated sugar

2 tsp salt

Preparation time
2–3 hours

1 Place the mackerel fillets in a large bowl, and pour over the salt. Gently rub the mackerel fillets with the salt, ensuring they are evenly covered.

2 Place the fillets on a bamboo strainer or in a colander. Leave for at least 30 minutes, preferably an hour, to allow juices drawn out by the salt to drain off. Rinse under cold running water, and pat dry with paper towels.

3 Mix together the vinegar, mirin or sugar, and salt in a plastic or glass bowl large enough to hold the fillets. Add the mackerel to the bowl and set aside to marinate for 1–2 hours.

4 Take the fillets out of the vinegar mixture, and pat dry with paper towels. The flesh should have whitened. Slowly peel off the papery thin outer skin, starting at the head. Don't worry if some of the iridescent underskin also comes off.

5 Place the fillets on a cutting board, and run the tips of your fingers lightly up and down them to feel for any small bones. Use tweezers to remove any that you find, and a sharp knife to trim and shape the fillets, if necessary.

Tenderizing fish skin
for sushi

Medium-sized scaly fish such as red snapper, sea bass, and silver bream have quite tough skin that needs to be blanched in order to tenderize it. The technique is called *matsukawa zukuri*, or the "pine bark method," since the fish skin shrinks a little when blanched and is said to resemble the bark of pine trees. Blanching the skin also gives the fish a sweeter flavor. Use any size fish fillet, but it must be scaled first [see p72].

> **Special equipment**
> *bamboo strainer or colander*
> *fukin or dish towel*
>
> **Preparation time**
> 10 minutes

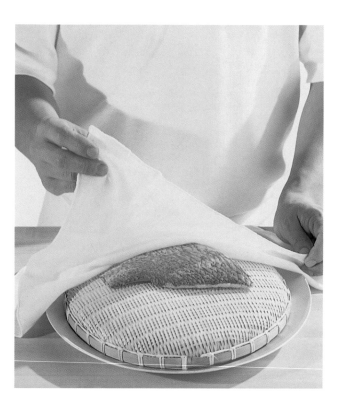

1 Place the scaled fillet skin-side-up on a bamboo strainer set over a shallow dish, and cover with a clean *fukin* or dish towel. Alternatively, place the fillet in a colander in the sink and cover.

2 Bring 10fl oz [300ml] of water to a boil. Carefully pour the freshly boiled water over the covered fillet.

3 Cool the fillet by plunging it into cold water or by holding it under cold-running water. The flesh should have whitened and the skin shrunk.

4 For scattered sushi or sashimi, slice the fillet into strips about ½ in [1cm] thick.

Shellfish and roe
kai rui

It is imperative that you buy the freshest fish for sushi and sashimi, and the same applies to shellfish. Ideally, shellfish such as crab, lobster, shrimp, prawns, scallops, oysters, and abalone should be bought while still alive, although this isn't always possible or practical. Shellfish can live for up to two days if kept in shallow water at a temperature of 35–40°F [5–6°C]. Check the following to ensure freshness:

• Shrimp and prawns in particular should be active and clear gray in color.
If no longer alive, select ones with clear, distinctive body markings.

• Scallops, oysters, and abalone should not float and should feel heavy; their shells should remain tightly closed and not be chipped.

• If buying a whole octopus, check that the eyes are clear and bright, not cloudy.

• Sea urchin is almost always bought already prepared, removed from its spiky shell. It should be mustard-colored, moist, and firm, not grayish yellow and slimy.

• Fish roes tend to have longer shelf-lives because they are often sold in jars or cans, which make them good pantry ingredients for sushi.

< Octopus is rarely sold whole outside Japan. Only the tentacles are used for sushi.

> It takes a firm hand to pry the precious oyster from its shell, but it makes a delicate topping for battleship sushi.

Crab
kani

Whatever the local variety may be, at a sushi bar, crab is always served cooked and referred to as *kani*. The "California roll," an invention originally created for American palates, uses cooked crabmeat, avocado, and mayonnaise in an inside-out rolled sushi. If the thought of buying a live crab and boiling it whole is too daunting, buy it already boiled or, better still, buy a dressed crab for making sushi at home.

white, coral-flecked crabmeat

Cooked crab
It takes some effort to extract the meat from a cooked crab – only white crabmeat is used for sushi.

Availability
Crabs come into season in Europe between April and December and in Australia, during spring and summer. Available throughout the year in North America, they are best in fall and winter. Frozen white meat can be used for sushi, but beware of "crab sticks" – actually cheap, processed white fish, not crab.

Crab claws contain sweet, white meat and are bigger on male crabs.

Females have larger "aprons" under their body and their meat is said to be sweeter than that of male crabs.

Preparing crab
for sushi

Whole cooked crabs are usually available at fish counters but it is easy to cook a fresh crab at home. Place the live crab in a large pot of cold salted water. Put the lid on, bring quickly to a boil, and cook for five to six minutes per 1lb [500g]. Drain the crab, cool, and extract the meat as below. Only white meat is used for sushi, not the more strongly flavored brown meat.

Special equipment
claw cracker or nutcracker

seafood pick or skewer

Preparation time
15–20 minutes
[excluding cooking time]

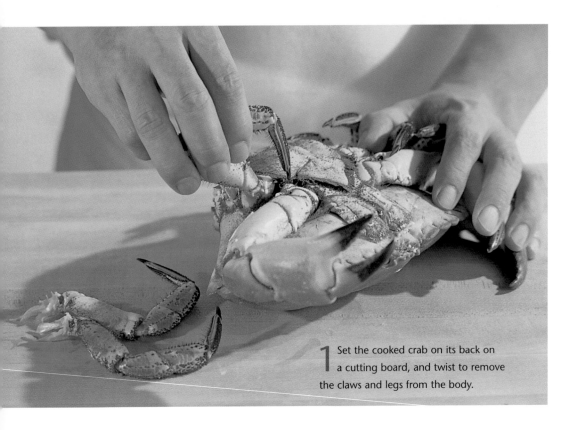

1 Set the cooked crab on its back on a cutting board, and twist to remove the claws and legs from the body.

2 Use a claw cracker or nutcracker to crack open the large claws. All the crab's legs will contain some meat, although the very small legs will hardly be worth the effort.

3 Flake the meat from the cracked claws using a seafood pick or skewer.

4 Using the heel of a knife, firmly cut through the spot where the crab's tail meets the body.

5 Ease the main part of the crab's body out of the shell.

6 Most of the white meat is found in the body of the crab, while the brown meat is in the shell.

7 The brown meat and red coral can easily be scraped from the shell if desired. Be sure to discard the pale paperlike head sac and stomach found just behind the crab's mouth.

8 Remove and discard the gray-looking gills or "dead man's fingers" from the sides of the central body section.

9 Pull the tail flap or apron from the main body section.

10 Using a heavy knife, cut the body in half to get to the meat.

11 Clean away any remaining coral or brown meat using a seafood pick or skewer.

12 Carefully pick the white meat out of all the sections of body, discarding any small pieces of membrane or shell.

13 If necessary, cut the body into quarters to enable you to reach all the inaccessible areas and remove the white meat.

Lobster
i s e   e b i

Revered as the king of the prawn family, the lobster's
high price reflects its high rank. Although it is not
considered a traditional Japanese sushi ingredient, its
firm flesh and excellent flavor have made it popular
with innovative sushi chefs outside of Japan. There
are two types of lobster – those with large claws and
those without, known as spiny lobsters. Both can
vary in length from 12–32 in [30–80cm] and weigh
as much as 6 lb [3kg]. Buy small to medium-sized
lobsters since larger ones tend to have drier, less
succulent flesh and blander flavor.

Turn the lobster
over and check
that the tail is
filled with meat.

Cooked lobster
Lobsters come in a wide variety
of colors but they all turn a
deep burgundy red when
properly cooked.

most of the
meat is in
the tail

Choose lobsters
with the least
barnacles.

Claws should feel
heavy and solid.

Spiny lobsters have two
large antennae instead
of claws.

Availability

Australia and North America are renowned as good sources of lobster. They come into season in Australia from mid-November to June. They are available year-round in North America, but are generally at their best between October and May; Maine, in the US, is a good source during the summer months. They come into season in Europe between April and November.

Preparing lobster
for sushi

Like crabs, lobsters contain white and brown meat, but only the white meat is used in sushi. If buying a live lobster, choose a lively one that feels heavy for its size. To cook it, put it in a large pan of cold salted water and bring it to a boil with the lid on. Cook for five to six minutes per 1lb [500g]. Alternatively, buy a pre-cooked lobster. Follow the steps below to extract the meat.

Special equipment

heavy knife or nutcracker

seafood pick or skewer

Preparation time
10–15 minutes
[excluding cooking time]

2 Use the heel of a heavy knife blade to crack open the claws, or alternatively, use a nutcracker. Pick out the meat with a seafood pick or skewer.

1 Most of the white meat is found in the muscular tail and, for clawed lobsters, in the two large claws.

3 Grasp the lobster in both hands and detach the head where it joins the body.

4 Using a sharp, heavy knife, cut through the translucent shell covering the bottom of the tail on both sides, at the point where it meets the upper shell.

5 Pull away and discard the translucent covering to get to the meat.

6 Pull the white meat out of the tail – it should come out in one large piece.

Prawns and shrimp
ebi

There are many varieties and sizes of prawns, both wild and farmed; smaller prawns are classified as shrimp. For sushi, both prawns and shrimp are referred to as *ebi*. They are usually served cooked and have a delicate flavor and a firm texture. Raw shrimp, *ama ebi*, is considered a great delicacy among sushi connoisseurs. A cleaned, raw shrimp has a jewel-like, glossy, almost transparent, appearance and is sweet in flavor with a tender texture. Demand for both prawns and shrimp is more than wild supplies can meet, so even sushi bars in Japan import frozen *ebi* from other parts of Asia.

The Mediterranean prawn is pink even when raw.

Mediterranean Prawn

The tiger shrimp has characteristic dark gray stripes on its body.

Tiger Shrimp

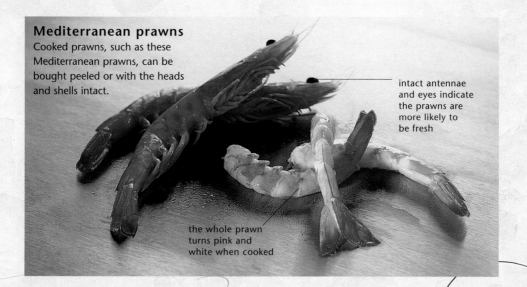

Mediterranean prawns
Cooked prawns, such as these
Mediterranean prawns, can be
bought peeled or with the heads
and shells intact.

intact antennae
and eyes indicate
the prawns are
more likely to
be fresh

the whole prawn
turns pink and
white when cooked

Availability
As a general rule, prawns
that live in warmer waters
are larger. Fresh prawns are
generally available in Europe
year-round. In the US,
excellent quality shrimp
are caught off the Maine
coast, especially between
November and March.
Australia probably has
the widest variety of large
prawns – they come into
season in April and last until
the end of November. The
raw shrimp, *ama ebi*, are best
bought already prepared from
Japanese specialty stores.

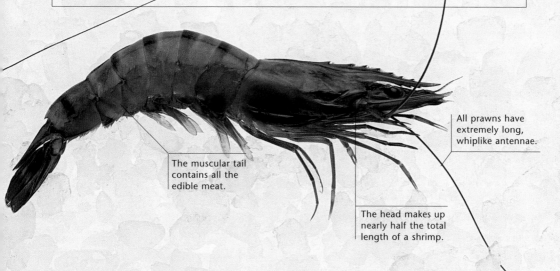

All prawns have
extremely long,
whiplike antennae.

The muscular tail
contains all the
edible meat.

The head makes up
nearly half the total
length of a shrimp.

Preparing shrimp
for sushi

Their firm sweet flesh makes king and tiger prawns popular ingredients in all types of sushi. Inserting a skewer along the underside before cooking prevents it from curling. Be careful not to overcook shrimp – this can give them a rubbery texture.

Special equipment
bamboo skewers

Preparation time
10 minutes

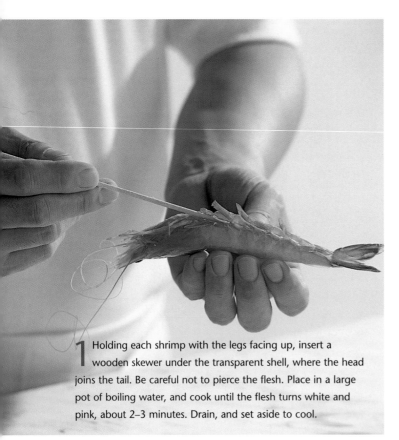

1 Holding each shrimp with the legs facing up, insert a wooden skewer under the transparent shell, where the head joins the tail. Be careful not to pierce the flesh. Place in a large pot of boiling water, and cook until the flesh turns white and pink, about 2–3 minutes. Drain, and set aside to cool.

2 Remove the skewer from the shrimp. Gently but firmly, pull the head to separate it from the body. Discard the head.

3 Holding the shrimp with the legs facing up, use your thumbs to remove the legs and peel away the outer shell. Leave the tail intact.

4 Using a sharp knife, cut along the underside of the shrimp until you reach the dark vein that runs the length of its body.

5 Use a knife or the wooden skewer to scrape out the dark vein. You may need to wipe any remaining vein away with a damp cloth.

6 Trim and neaten the ends of the tail for an elegant presentation. For some sushi, such as hand-formed sushi, you might want to carefully pull off the tail shell.

Squid and octopus
ika / tako

The Japanese word *ika* refers to many different varieties of squid, but *ma ika* and *yari ika* are most preferred for sushi. Always buy squid fresh, if possible; it freezes well if you have too much, which makes it a convenient ingredient for home sushi-making. The octopus feeds on other sushi ingredients such as crab, lobster, and scallops – this gourmet diet makes it high in protein and gives it excellent flavor. It has a firm texture and makes a very good sushi topping. Larger octopus have thicker tentacles which are easier to slice for hand-formed sushi [p116–7].

Squid

The body and tentacles are used to make many different types of sushi.

Octopus

Fresh squid

Its pearly white, glossy flesh has
a sticky, almost resistant texture.
Squid is nearly always served raw.

Cooked octopus

For sushi, octopus is boiled,
which tenderizes and firms
the flesh. Its gray skin turns
burgundy, and its flesh whitens.

Only the octopus's
tentacles are used
as a sushi topping.

Availability

Squid and octopus
are widely available
year-round, which
makes them good
sushi and sashimi
ingredients.
However, squid is at
its best in Europe in
fall and winter, and
during spring in
North America.
Octopus is generally
at its best during
winter and spring
in the northern
hemisphere.

Look for squid and
octopus that still
have their tentacles
intact and most of
their skin on – these
are signs that they
have been handled
well. Fresh seafood
should smell like the
ocean, never fishy,
and look shiny and
firm. High quality
frozen squid or
octopus is much
better than low
quality fresh.

Preparing squid
for sushi

A popular sushi ingredient, squid is extremely simple to clean. Choose only the freshest squid – it should look glossy and have shiny black eyes. Use the method below to prepare squid for Scattered Sushi [p132–49] or Hand-formed Sushi [p208–17]. For Stuffed Squid Sushi [p154–7], keep the body and tentacles intact.

Special equipment

clean cloth or dish towel

Preparation time
10 minutes

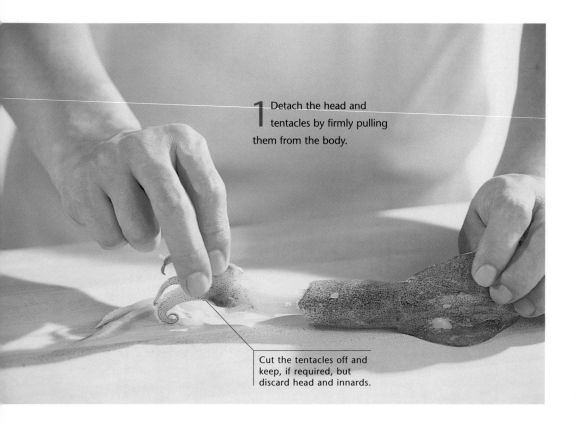

1 Detach the head and tentacles by firmly pulling them from the body.

Cut the tentacles off and keep, if required, but discard head and innards.

2 Pull the translucent, quill-shaped piece of cartilage out of the body and discard it.

3 If stuffing the squid, keep the body whole. Otherwise, insert a sharp knife into the body and carefully slit it down one side.

4 Either open the body and lay it flat, skin-side-up, or lay the intact body on a clean surface or cutting board. Grasp the two triangular fins and pull upward. Discard the fins and the skin.

5 Use a clean, damp cloth to wipe away the mucus lining on one side and any pieces of skin left behind on the other. If using the squid whole, turn it inside-out and wipe with a cloth.

Preparing octopus
for sushi

Although the whole of an octopus can be eaten raw, normally only the boiled tentacles are used for sushi. Boiling tenderizes the meat and gives it a sweet flavor, but keep the heat as low as possible since rapid boiling toughens it. Fresh octopus needs to be rubbed clean with salt before cooking. Clean the suckers and ends of the tentacles because they may contain mud or sand.

Special equipment

1 cup [7oz/200g] salt, or enough to coat the tentacles

bamboo strainer or colander

Preparation time
45 minutes

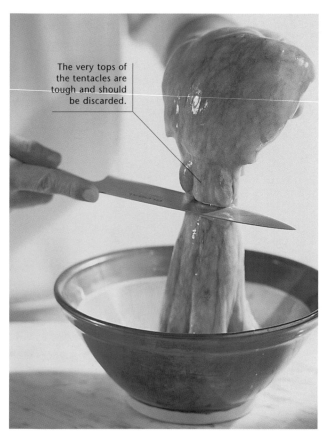

The very tops of the tentacles are tough and should be discarded.

1 Using a sharp knife, cut the tentacles off just below the eyes.

2 Put the tentacles in a bowl or on a cutting board and pour the salt over. Rub the salt into the tentacles to tenderize and clean them.

3 Bring a large pan of salted water to a boil, and add the tentacles. Bring back to a boil, then reduce the heat and simmer gently for about 10 minutes.

4 Drain the tentacles in a bamboo strainer or colander, and set aside to cool. The skin should have turned a deep pink and the tentacles curled tightly, showing clean white suckers.

5 Cut the tentacles away from the central section which contains the octopus's mouth parts or "beak." This section should be discarded.

6 With the blade of the knife at a 45° angle to the cutting board, cut the tentacles diagonally into ⅛ in [3–4mm] slices.

Abalone, oysters, scallops
awabi / kaki / hotate gai

One of the earliest ingredients to be used in sushi, abalone is also one of the most highly prized and expensive. It has a unique, subtle flavor and chewy flesh that doesn't appeal to everybody. Oysters, eaten raw even outside of Japan, have a light salty flavor. They are usually served as a topping for Battleship Sushi [p218–21]. The delicately flavored flesh of the scallop is served as a topping for Hand-Formed Sushi [p208–17]; smaller scallops are served on battleship sushi.

Abalone

Abalone can grow up to 1ft [30cm] wide, but the larger they are the more rubbery their flesh.

Look for a yellow tag, which shows that it is farmed.

The shell is lined with mother-of-pearl shell.

Fresh oysters should always be firmly closed.

Availability

The Japanese love abalone and since demand far exceeds the wild supply, it is commercially cultivated. Only buy abalone with the yellow tags that show it has been farmed – wild it is a protected species. In Japan, it is available year-round, but is best between April and June. In North America, it is found off the Pacific coast. Oysters can be eaten year-round, but they tend to be less flavorful from May to August when they spawn. Scallops are widely available all around the world and are also commercially farmed.

Oyster shells are often dotted with barnacles.

Scallops

Fresh shellfish close their shells sharply when tapped.

Oysters

All of the watery gray body of the oyster is edible.

Only the scallop's large white muscle is used for sushi.

Preparing abalone
for sushi

In Japan, abalone is considered a delicacy, but many non-Japanese sushi lovers can't get excited about it because they find it bland and chewy. The best way to enjoy its texture and delicate flavor is to eat it raw and to slice it as thinly as possible.

> ### Special equipment
>
> *oyster knife or any short, strong knife*
>
> *clean cloth or dish towel*
>
> *small brush for cleaning shellfish*
>
> ### Preparation time
> 45 minutes

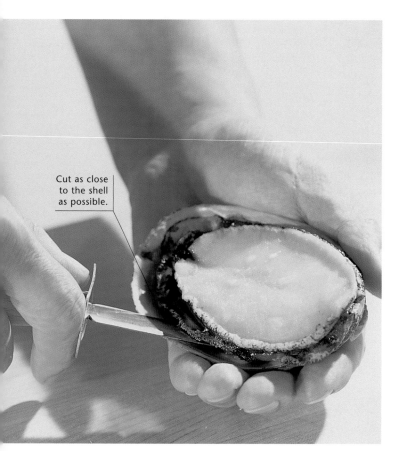

Cut as close to the shell as possible.

1 Slide an oyster knife or short, strong knife under the abalone in the shell, and cut the attached muscle.

2 Carefully pull off the dark intestines and discard. Wipe clean with a damp cloth.

3 Cut out the mouth at the slightly thinner end of the abalone and discard.

4 Trim off the dark fringe with a knife and discard. Wash the abalone under cold, running water, scrubbing off any mucus with a brush.

5 Slice the abalone horizontally into ⅛ in [3–4mm] slices and use for hand-formed sushi, scattered sushi, or sashimi.

Preparing oysters and scallops for sushi

Because of their runny consistency, oysters are used in Battleship Sushi [see p218–21]. Thin slices of raw scallop, which have a delicate sweet flavor, are used as a topping for Hand-Formed Sushi [see p208–17] and for Scattered Sushi [see p132–49]. Discard oysters and scallops with cracked, chipped, or broken shells.

Special equipment

oyster knife or any thin, sharp knife

dish towel

Preparation time
about 1 minute per
oyster or scallop

Shucking oysters

1 Place the oyster on a firm surface. Use a towel to protect your hand from the sharp shell. Work the knife into the hinge, the narrowest point of the shell. Twist the blade to separate the shells slightly. Slide the blade into the oyster shell, keeping it flat against the upper shell, and scrape it from one side to the other to cut the muscle. The upper shell can now easily be removed.

2 Cut through the muscle that attaches the oyster to the lower shell, and carefully remove the oyster. Use immediately.

Shelling scallops

1 Slide an oyster knife or a thin, sharp knife into the shell and cut the muscle that attaches the upper and lower shells. Keep the blade flat against the upper shell and work the blade from side to side.

2 Noting the position of the cut part of the muscle, insert the blade under the scallop at the same spot and cut through the muscle attaching the scallop to the lower shell.

3 Tear off the fringe and bright orange coral – only the round, white muscle is used for sushi.

4 Rinse in cold water and cut into thin slices about ⅛ in [3–4mm] thick by cutting across the top of the scallop. Use immediately.

Fish roe, caviar and sea urchin

Because of their unmanageable nature, fish roe and caviar are usually served in the form of battleship-shaped sushi, where a sheet of nori holds the topping in place. Some of the smaller roes, such as flying fish roe, or *tobiko*, are used as coatings to add color to inside-out rolled sushi. Fish roe and caviar are considered to be delicacies and often command exorbitant prices. Herring roe, or *kazunoko*, for example, was once so abundant on the coasts of Japan that it was used as fertilizer. These days it is so expensive, it has earned the name "yellow diamond."

Flying Fish Roe

Known in Japanese as *tobiko*, these have a slightly crunchy texture and burst in your mouth when you bite into them.

Sevruga Caviar

The sushi conoisseur's favorite, sea urchin or *uni* has a subtle nutty flavor when fresh; freezing it can make it less palatable.

The eggs of the Sevruga sturgeon are small, gray, and often saltier in flavor than the other varieties.

Sea Urchin

Availability

Caviar and lumpfish caviar are widely available in small jars or tins. Caviar is expensive and, although not a traditional sushi ingredient, its silky texture and luxurious taste have made it popular among more innovative sushi chefs. Once opened, caviar should be refrigerated and used within a week. Salmon roe is available in small jars and can be soaked in sake for 1–2 minutes to separate the eggs. It should also be refrigerated once opened and used within a week. Japan and North America are the primary sources of sea urchin.

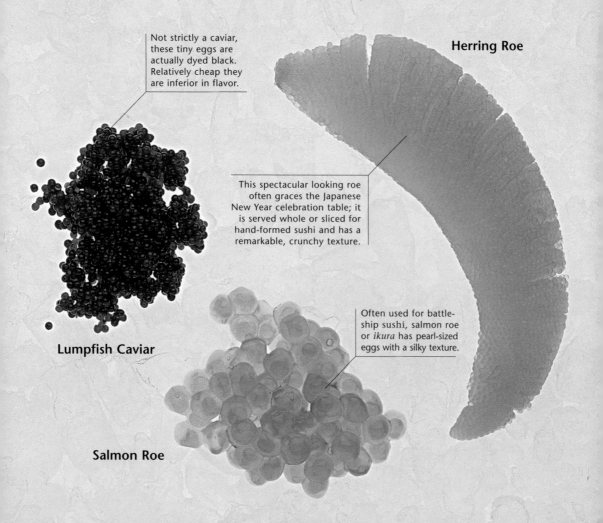

Not strictly a caviar, these tiny eggs are actually dyed black. Relatively cheap they are inferior in flavor.

Herring Roe

This spectacular looking roe often graces the Japanese New Year celebration table; it is served whole or sliced for hand-formed sushi and has a remarkable, crunchy texture.

Lumpfish Caviar

Often used for battle-ship sushi, salmon roe or *ikura* has pearl-sized eggs with a silky texture.

Salmon Roe

Other seafood
for sushi

Sushi has a wide variety of toppings and fillings, some familiar and some more unusual than others. You may first come across some of the fish, shellfish, and other seafood listed here in sushi bars, but as you become more confident with sushi-making, consider using some of the following to broaden your range.

Common clam [asari]

The small common clam is not usually used in sushi but is often added to soups [see p238]. They live on the seabed and as a result can contain grit. To clean the grit from clams, put them in a large bowl with a tablespoon of salt, a handful of cornmeal, and enough water to cover them. Refrigerate for two hours, then rinse before use.

Venus clam [hamaguri]

Larger than the common clam, about 3in [8cm], the venus clam is available year-round. Like most other shellfish, it is best in winter and spring. Its yellow-tinged flesh has a delicate sweet flavor and is often eaten raw in sushi.

Round clam [baka gai]

This small red clam is about the same size as the ark shell [aka gai] and tastes very similar. It used to be boiled before eating, but nowadays it is served raw as

< Clams can be an elegant addition to a simple clear soup, but they need to be cleaned first.

a topping for hand-formed sushi. The adductor muscle, which opens the shell, is as delicious as the body of the clam and is a highly praised delicacy served in battleship-style sushi.

Horse clam [miru gai]

This large hard-shell clam is commonly found in the coastal waters off Japan and is also plentiful on the west coast of North America. Although the main body is edible, it is rather watery and only suitable for clam chowder or stuffing – it is the long, muscular siphon that protrudes from its shell that is used for sushi and sashimi. It is pale peach in color and has a subtle flavor. Preparation of *miru gai* is best left to the trained sushi chef and is not for the faint hearted. In order to prove its freshness, the sushi chef wacks the clam against the counter to see if it retracts its siphon – he then quickly slices it off.

Mantis shrimp [shako]

This odd-looking relation of the prawn and crab grows to about 6in [15cm] in length. It is common in the coastal waters around Japan. For sushi, it is shelled and boiled, then brushed with

∧ Buy round clams and other rarer varieties of seafood from Japanese fish markets.

a thick, sweet soy-based sauce. It is crunchy with a nutty flavor and is a popular topping for hand-formed sushi.

Garfish [sayori]

This small slender fish has a silver body and a long beak and measures less than 16in [40cm]. Its transparent white flesh has a delicate sweet flavor. Traditionally it was marinated and not really used in hand-formed sushi in Japan before World War II. Today, you are likely to see it served as a topping for hand-formed sushi and also as elegant sashimi.

∧ Crack open the huge legs of the Alaskan king crab to get to the succulent meat inside.

Alaskan king crab [kani]

These large crabs are available pre-cooked from most good fishsellers, but tend to be more expensive than other varieties. The legs, which need to be cracked open, contain more of the sweet, white and red meat than the body. Alaskan crab makes a good topping for hand-formed sushi and

is often held in place with a strip of nori. Buy fresh crabmeat if possible, but frozen is also available.

Freshwater eel [unagi]

Grilled eel is traditionally eaten on the Day of the Cow – the Japanese believe that it keeps them healthy for the rest of the year and nearly 1,000 tons of it are consumed over the 24-hour period. Freshwater eel is never eaten raw, even in sushi. It is filleted and steamed first; then cut into small pieces; skewered; and dipped in a sweet sauce of reduced eel stock, sugar, and soy sauce. It is then grilled over a charcoal fire. Most of the *unagi* found in sushi bars is imported ready-made from Japan. It has a rich, nutty flavor and is very tender. Ready-made *unagi* is available vacuum-packed from Japanese food stores.

Conger eel [anago]

This sea eel grows much bigger than its freshwater cousin – up to 10ft [3m] in length – but it is best eaten when it is younger and smaller. Preparing *anago* is a highly skilled job and is considered a good test of the quality of a sushi bar. Preparation is similar to that of the freshwater eel. *Anago* is a popular sushi ingredient, but its flesh is leaner than *unagi* so not as rich in flavor. Conger eel is widely available year-round.

Dover sole [shita birame]

The Japanese name means "tongue" – an apt description of this odd-looking fish with its disproportionately small head and tapering tail. It grows to no more than 1ft [30cm] in length, but it has a wonderfully delicate flavor and texture. It is available year-round except in April.

Yellowtail [hamachi]

These sleek migratory fish cruise around the open sea. Yellowtail is the common name for a specific type of amberjack. The Japanese variety has light golden flesh and very little fat. *Hamachi* is best eaten young when its rich, smooth, buttery texture and slightly smoky flavor can be fully enjoyed. The meat around the pectoral fins, just behind the gills, is considered the best and, in a sushi bar, is often reserved for special customers. It is used for hand-formed sushi in Japan; some sushi connoisseurs prefer it to tuna.

Swordfish [makajiki]

Its rarity and exquisitely flavored pink flesh make swordfish one of the most sought after sushi ingredients in Japan. There are several different varieties available: *makajiki* [swordfish], *mekajiki* [broadbill], and *shirokawa* and *kurokawa*, which do not have English names. The most highly regarded of all is *makajiki*, a handsome fish that can grow to 6½ ft [2m]. *Makajiki* comes into season in Japan in the fall. It can be difficult to buy swordfish fresh enough for sushi outside Japan. Beware of gray, watery steaks with gaps in the flesh.

∨ Most swordfish steaks at fish counters are not of high enough quality for sushi.

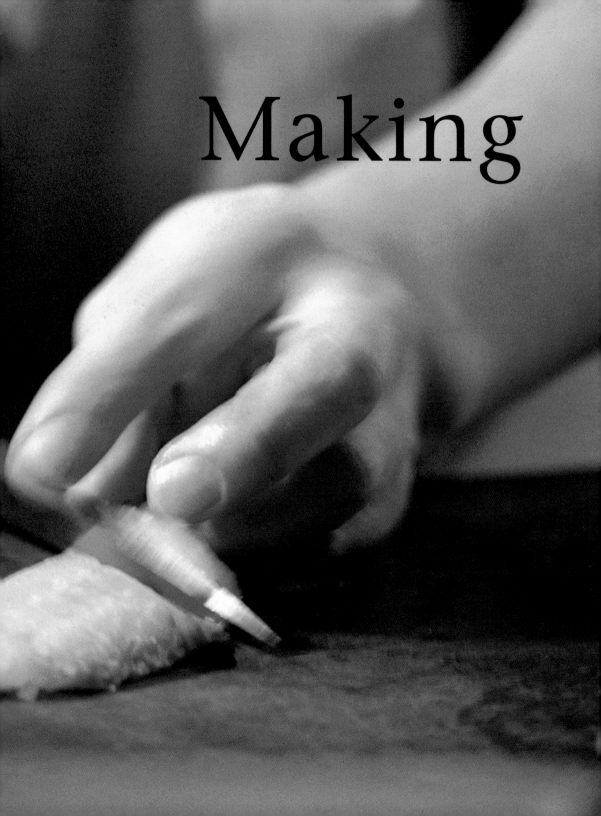

Making

Scattered sushi
chirashi zushi

This is the easiest type of sushi to prepare. It makes a satisfying one-course meal and is served either in individual bowls or brought to the table on a larger plate. *Chirashi* means "to scatter" and rather than shaping the rice as with other types of sushi, ingredients such as fish and vegetables are arranged on top of it or mixed into it.

There are two basic types of scattered sushi. *Edomae chirashi zushi,* or Tokyo-style sushi, consists of a few slices of sashimi-cut fish decoratively arranged on a bed of sushi rice [see p134–7]. For *gomoko zushi,* or Kansai-style sushi, the ingredients are often cooked and mixed together with the sushi rice [see p138–9]. This is the most versatile form of sushi and something closer to a rice salad, so experiment and use the recipes that follow as guidelines rather than following them strictly.

As with all sushi, start cooking the rice first and then prepare the rest of your ingredients. At the end, the actual assembly takes very little time at all. Please note, the preparation times in the recipes that follow do not include the time that it takes to prepare the rice because it is so easy to make in advance.

< Save time when making sushi by preparing your ingredients in advance.

> Tokyo-style sushi [see p134–7] – an artistic arrangement of fish and vegetables on a bed of rice.

Tokyo-style sushi
edomae chirashi zushi

Originally, this dish would have been a simple one-course meal – a bowl of rice topped with a few slices of raw fish and whatever vegetables were fresh that day. It was popular in Edo, which is now Tokyo. There is no strict rule regarding what seafood to use – try to combine good colors and textures. Unlike many other scattered sushi, *edomae chirashi zushi* is best served in individual bowls. Arrange the ingredients however you like, but try to mix shapes and colors. To speed assembly, prepare ingredients beforehand.

Ingredients

1 quantity prepared sushi rice [p36–8]

4 tbsp shredded daikon or cucumber

4 perilla leaves or sprouts to garnish

1 skinless fillet of tuna, about 5oz [150g], cut for sashimi [p89] into 12 slices

1 thick Japanese omelette [p40–43], cut into 8 strips, ½ in [1cm] thick

1 medium squid body, about 3oz [90g], cleaned [p114–15] and cut into 4 strips

1 skinless fillet of salmon, about 5oz [150g], cut for sashimi [p89] into 8 slices

4 prepared tiger shrimp [p110–11]

1 vinegar-marinated mackerel fillet [p92–3] about 4oz [120g], cut into 8 slices

4 scallops, cut in half

4 white fish roses made using 4oz [120g] skinless fillet of white fish [p242]

4 tsp salmon roe

4 wasabi paste leaves made with 4 tsp paste [p51]

1 baby cucumber, cut into pine branch garnishes [p50]

Serves 4

Preparation time
1 hour

1 Fill each bowl two-thirds full with sushi rice. Place a small, loose ball of shredded daikon or cucumber against one side of each bowl; lean a perilla leaf against it; or use sprouts.

2 Position 3 slices of tuna and 2 pieces of omelette in front of the perilla leaf or sprouts.

3 Curl each piece of squid, and place in front of the omelette. Arrange 2 slices of salmon next to the tuna.

4 Cut a shrimp so that it folds in half and add it to the arrangement.

5 Arrange 2 slices of mackerel with silver skin showing, 2 scallop halves, and a white fish rose in the bowl.

6 Add a spoonful of salmon roe, and finally, garnish with a wasabi leaf and a cucumber pine branch.

Tokyo-style scattered sushi – a feast for the mouth and for the eyes.

Vegetarian scattered sushi
gomoko zushi

This is one of the easiest types of sushi to prepare at home. In Japan it is made with the excess of whatever vegetables are found in the refrigerator. You could add asparagus to this dish – I've even been known to throw in a handful of frozen peas. It makes an ideal lunch dish, is great for picnics, and can even be served as a light dinner party appetizer. Save time by preparing the shiitake mushrooms, kampyo, and tofu pouches in advance.

1   Steam or blanch the snow peas until tender, about 4–5 minutes. Reserve a few whole snow peas to use as a garnish and chop the rest.

2   Spread the rice in the bottom of a large serving dish, or divide between 4 individual bowls. Keep the rice as loose as possible.

3   Scatter the shiitake mushroom slices, the kampyo, and the tofu pouch slices over the rice.

4   Set aside a few slices of lotus root and a few carrot flowers to use as a garnish. Add the remaining lotus root slices, the carrot flowers, and the chopped snow peas.

5   Cut the omelette into fine shreds and scatter over the rice. Garnish with the slices of lotus root and the reserved carrot flowers and snow peas.

6   Sprinkle with the shredded nori just before serving. Add this at the very last minute, otherwise it can get soggy.

Ingredients

1oz [30g] snow peas

1 quantity prepared sushi rice [p36–8]

4 large seasoned shiitake mushrooms [p31], thinly sliced

1oz [30g] prepared kampyo [p30], chopped into 1in [2cm] lengths

2 seasoned deep-fried tofu pouches [p46], unseparated, thinly sliced

2oz [60g] lotus root, thinly sliced

1 carrot, cut into flowers [p48]

3–4 thin Japanese omelettes [p44–5]

2 sheets nori seaweed, thinly shredded

Serves 4

Preparation time
40 minutes

Vegetarian scattered sushi – a mix of flavors, textures, and colors.

Asparagus and scrambled egg sushi

I like to serve this sushi in the spring when asparagus comes into season, but you can make it at any time of year and use whatever green vegetable is in season.

1 Steam the asparagus for 2–3 minutes. Reserve the tips to use as a garnish, and chop the stalks into small pea-sized pieces.
2 Mix the sushi rice and chopped asparagus stalks together in a large mixing bowl, and spread the mixture in a large serving dish or divide between 4 individual bowls.
3 Scatter the scrambled egg over the rice and garnish with the asparagus tips.

Ingredients

1lb [500g] asparagus, trimmed

1 quantity prepared sushi rice [p36–8]

1 quantity scrambled eggs [p43]

Serves 4

Preparation time
40 minutes

Snow peas and vine-ripened tomato sushi

This is an excellent light lunch in the summer. The combination of slightly crunchy bright green snow peas and sweet, succulent vine-ripened tomatoes is quite refreshing.

1 Blanch the snow peas and cool immediately in cold water. Reserve a few whole snow peas to use as a garnish, and cut the remaining ones into thin strips.
2 Mix the sushi rice with the snow pea strips and chopped tomatoes in a large mixing bowl. Spread the mixture in a large serving dish, or divide between 4 individual bowls.
3 Sprinkle over the toasted sesame seeds and garnish with the reserved whole snow peas.

Ingredients

5oz [150g] snow peas

1 quantity prepared sushi rice [p36–8]

5oz [150g] vine-ripened tomatoes, seeded and finely chopped

1 tbsp toasted sesame seeds

Serves 4

Preparation time
40 minutes

Fresh seasonal vegetables add a delicious bite to scattered sushi.

Broccoli and shredded omelette sushi

Be careful to steam the broccoli only briefly to help retain its vibrant color and its crunchiness.

1   Cut the broccoli into small, bite-size pieces. Steam for 2 minutes, then set aside to cool.
2   Cut the omelettes into fine shreds. Mix the sushi rice, broccoli, and shredded omelette in a large bowl.
3   Transfer the rice mixture to a large serving dish, or divide between 4 individual plates and scatter the broccoli on top.
4   Place a small mound of ginger on top of the rice. Sprinkle over the seasame seeds before serving.

Ingredients

1lb [500g] purple broccoli or rapini, tough stems removed

4 thin omelettes [p44–5]

1 quantity prepared sushi rice [p36–8]

4 tbsp shredded red or pink pickled ginger

2 tbsp toasted sesame seeds

Serves 4

Preparation time
40 minutes

Mushroom and egg sushi

Mushroom and egg complement each other perfectly in this dish. Use fresh enoki, shiitake, or oyster mushrooms.

1   Heat the oil in a large frying pan or wok, and stir-fry the mushrooms for 2 minutes. Remove from the heat, add the soy sauce, and stir gently for 30 seconds longer. Drain and set aside.
2   Combine the sushi rice with the cooked mushrooms and sesame seeds in a large bowl.
3   Transfer the rice mixture to a large serving dish, or divide between 4 individual plates. Cut the omelettes into fine shreds, then sprinkle over the rice. Garnish with the shredded nori just before serving.

Ingredients

2 tbsp vegetable oil

1lb [500g] mushrooms, sliced into ½ in [1cm] strips

1 tbsp soy sauce

1 quantity prepared sushi rice [p36–8]

2 tbsp toasted sesame seeds

4 thin omelettes [p44–5]

shredded nori to garnish

Serves 4

Preparation time
40 minutes

Pink pickled ginger tops broccoli and shredded omelette sushi.

Sun-dried tomato and mozzarella sushi

My parents would be horrified by this fusion sushi – or what they would call "confusion sushi," but it really works.

1   Mix the sushi rice, sun-dried tomatoes, and mozzarella cheese together in a large mixing bowl.
2   Transfer the rice mixture to a large serving dish, or divide between 4 individual bowls.
3   Garnish with basil leaves and serve.

Ingredients

1 quantity prepared sushi rice [p36–8]

3½ oz [100g] sun-dried tomatoes, drained and sliced

6oz [175g] fresh mozzarella cheese, drained and cubed

large bunch of fresh basil leaves to garnish

Serves 4

Preparation time
30 minutes

Crabmeat, chile, and lime sushi

This is fusion sushi that combines fresh crab and chiles, two favorites of mine. Vary the amount of chile to suit your taste and add a little lime juice to help bring the contrasting flavors together. You might find it more economical to buy frozen white crabmeat.

1   Combine the prepared sushi rice, crabmeat, and chopped chiles in a large mixing bowl.
2   Cut each piece of nori to plate size, and lay a sheet on each plate.
3   Divide the rice mixture between the individual plates, piling it on top of the nori squares. Squeeze a little lime juice over the rice; garnish with the cilantro leaves and slices of lime, and serve.

Ingredients

1 quantity prepared sushi rice [p36–8]

6oz [175g] crabmeat

2–4 large red chiles, seeded and finely chopped

4 sheets nori seaweed

juice of 1 lime

fresh cilantro leaves and slices of lime to garnish

Serves 4

Preparation time
40 minutes

Garnish sun-dried tomato and mozzarella sushi with basil leaves.

Seared beef fillet and red onion sushi

This recipe uses the traditional Japanese method for cooking bonito fish, *tataki*, to cook beef, but it works just as well with tuna steak. The beef is briefly seared to seal in the flavor while the center remains almost rare. Submerging the seared beef in ice-cold water instantly halts the cooking process and also washes away excess fat. You can save time by preparing up to step 5 in advance. This is a robust dish that should be enjoyed with a full-bodied red wine.

Ingredients

1 medium red onion, peeled and halved

1lb [500g] beef fillet

1 tbsp vegetable oil

3½ floz [100ml] sake

3½ floz [100ml] soy sauce

1 quantity prepared sushi rice [p36–8]

2 scallions, finely chopped, to garnish

chile daikon relish [p33]

salt and freshly ground black pepper

Serves 4

Preparation time
1 hour 30 minutes

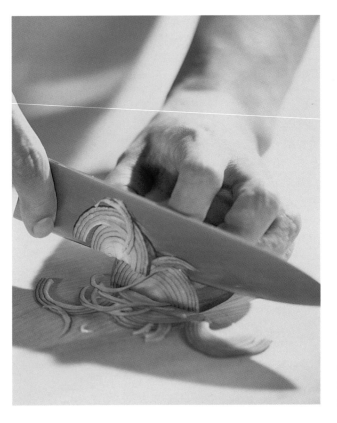

1 Cut the onion into thin slices and place in a bowl of cold water. Set aside to soak for 10 minutes. Pat the beef fillet dry with paper towel. Rub salt and pepper into it, and set aside to season for 30 minutes.

2 Heat the oil in a large heavy-bottomed skillet and sear the beef until brown, about 2 minutes on each side.

3 The surface of the beef should be well-browned, but the inside should be raw. However, you can cook the meat for longer if you prefer.

4 Transfer the beef to a bowl of iced water and leave to stand for 10 minutes. Combine the sake and soy in a shallow dish.

5 Wipe the beef dry with paper towel and transfer to the dish of sake and soy mixture. Set aside to marinate for at least 30 minutes, or leave to marinate overnight in the refrigerator.

7 Fill each bowl two-thirds full with sushi rice, and top with the slices of beef.

6 Remove the beef from the marinade and pat dry with paper towel. Cut into ¼ in [5 mm] slices or cut it as thinly as possible.

8 Drain the onion slices and use to garnish. Sprinkle the scallions over, and serve with chile daikon relish.

Seared beef fillet, an unconventional but delicious sushi ingredient.

Stuffed sushi
inari zushi

This form of sushi uses cooked ingredients such as a thin omelettes, cabbage leaves, or deep-fried tofu as a wrapping material for sushi rice and other cooked ingredients. Vegetarian stuffed sushi, especially the traditional *inari zushi* which is made with delicious pouches of seasoned deep-fried tofu, is great to take on a picnic – it is easy to transport and does not spoil too quickly.

The Japanese prepare stuffed sushi at home and eat the tasty little parcels under cherry trees in spring which are famous for their beautiful, fragrant blossom. The fillings can vary from simple plain sushi rice mixed with a few chopped fresh herbs to whatever seasonal ingredients are available. There are no strict rules as to what you can or cannot use – I have included a recipe for one of my personal favorites, stuffed squid sushi. Because most types of stuffed sushi can be prepared up to six hours in advance, it also makes a convenient party food.

< Cooked ingredients are mixed with rice and then used as a stuffing or wrapped to create a parcel.

> Deep-fried tofu makes a wonderful container for thinly sliced shiitake mushrooms and rice.

Stuffed tofu pouches
inari zushi

This conveniently portable form of sushi is a popular choice for sushi lunch boxes. The tofu pouches have a distinctive sweet and savory flavor and are also highly nutritious because of their soy content. The pouches taste delicious even with plain sushi rice but you can try adding other ingredients such as chopped perilla leaves or lemon zest.

1   Mix the sushi rice with the sesame seeds and mushrooms in a large mixing bowl. Carefully spoon the filling into each tofu pouch until the pouches are half-full.

2   Make a parcel by carefully folding one side of the tofu pouch under and then the other.

Ingredients

1 quantity prepared sushi rice [p36–8]

2 tbsp toasted sesame seeds

6 seasoned shiitake mushrooms [p31], very finely sliced

6 seasoned tofu pouches, [p46]

Makes 12 pieces

Preparation time
45 minutes

Use your fingers to loosely pack the filling; make sure you don't overfill the pouch.

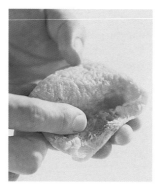

Carefully fold the edges over to make a parcel.

Stuffed tofu pouches with simple fillings make perfect picnic food.

Stuffed squid sushi
i k a   z u s h i

Here, squid is first cooked in a sweet vinegar mix – amazu – and then stuffed with a mixture of seasoned rice and vegetables. Experiment with different stuffings, but since *ika zushi* is always served sliced, use vegetables such as green beans, carrots, cucumbers, and chiles that add color.

Ingredients

for amazu:
3 tbsp Japanese rice vinegar

1 tbsp sugar

1 tsp salt

for squid:
2 medium squid with tentacles, about 10 oz [300 g] each, cleaned and body intact [p114–15]

1 tbsp soy sauce

2 oz [60 g] green beans, trimmed

1 quantity prepared sushi rice [p36–8]

2 in [5 cm] piece fresh ginger, grated

5 perilla leaves, chopped, or 2 tbsp chopped fresh cilantro leaves

Serves 4

Preparation time
1 hour

1 Mix the ingredients for the amazu together in a small bowl. Add to the squid with the soy sauce in a non-aluminum pan. Cook gently for 2–3 minutes.

2 Drain the squid and set
aside. Once cool enough
to handle, chop the tentacles.
Steam or blanch the green
beans until tender, about 2–3
minutes, then chop into small
pea-sized pieces.

3 Mix the sushi rice with the chopped green
beans, grated ginger, chopped tentacles, and
chopped perilla leaves or cilantro in a bowl.

4 Spoon the rice mixture into each of the
marinated squid bodies.

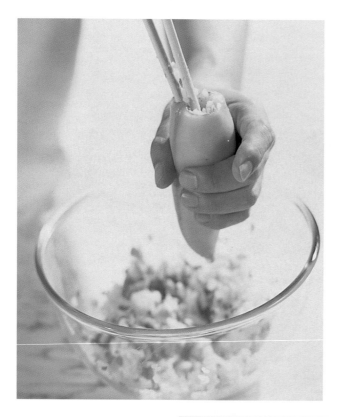

5 Gently pack the filling into the squid with a pair of cooking chopsticks or a spoon. Set aside to stand at room temperature for 30 minutes to an hour to allow the flavors to develop.

6 Use a sharp knife dipped in water to slice the stuffed squid into ¾ in [2cm] thick rounds. Arrange on a plate and serve.

Green beans and perilla leaves add color to stuffed squid.

Omelette parcels
fukusa zushi

A *fukusa* is a small handkerchief used in the traditional Japanese tea ceremony. It is folded in different ways as part of the ceremonial performance. Here, a thin Japanese omelette is folded into a parcel and stuffed with a filling of rice, shiitake mushrooms, and sesame seeds.

Ingredients

1 quantity prepared sushi rice [p36–8]

8 seasoned shiitake mushrooms [p31], thinly sliced

2 tbsp toasted sesame seeds

8 thin Japanese omelettes [p44–5]

8 strips of prepared kampyo [p30], 5 in [12 cm] long or 8 cilantro stems, leaves removed

Makes 8 parcels

Preparation time
1 hour 20 minutes

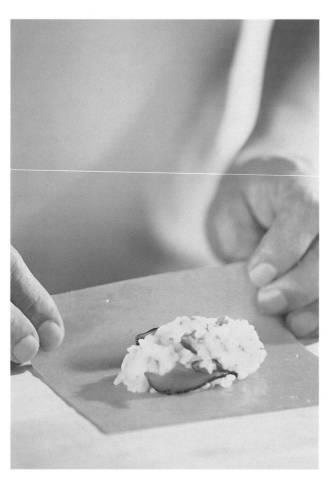

1 Mix the sushi rice with the shiitake mushrooms and sesame seeds in a bowl. Place an omelette on a clean surface or cutting board and cut the edges off it to make a square roughly 8 x 8in [20 x 20cm]. Spoon about 2 tablespoons of rice stuffing into the middle of the omelette square.

2 Position the omelette so that one corner faces you. Fold this lower corner over the filling to meet the top corner.

3 Then one after the other, fold in the side corners to meet at the center.

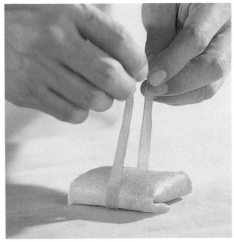

4 Now fold the omelette over the top corner to form a neat, rectangular parcel.

5 Use a strip of seasoned kampyo or a cilantro stem, tenderized by running the back of a knife along it, to tie the parcel.

Omelette purses
chakin zushi

Omelette makes a colorful wrapping material, and here each stuffed purse is tied together with a bright green cilantro stem. This sushi is popular with my vegetarian friends.

Ingredients

1 quantity prepared sushi rice [p36–8]

4 seasoned shiitake mushrooms [p31], thinly sliced

2 tbsp toasted sesame seeds

8 thin Japanese omelettes [p44–5]

8 cilantro or flat leaf parsely stems, leaves removed, 6 in [15 cm] long

Serves 4

Preparation time
1 hour 30 minutes

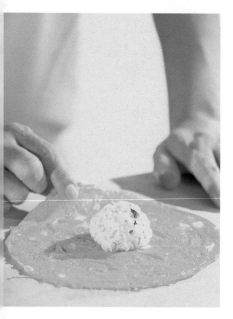

1 Mix the sushi rice with the shiitake mushrooms and sesame seeds in a bowl. Place an omelette on a clean surface or cutting board and spoon about 2 tablespoons of rice stuffing into the middle of it.

2 Run the back of a knife along the cilantro or flat leaf parsley stem to tenderize it. Gather up the edges of the omelette and tie together with the stem.

Purses and parcels can be tied with coriander stems or kampyo.

Savoy cabbage leaves with herb and egg rice

The bright green color and crinkled texture of savoy cabbage make it an interesting wrapping material. The leaves are blanched very briefly then immersed in cold water, which helps them to retain their color. Be sure to pat any excess water off the leaves, otherwise the stuffing can become soggy. Use the same technique to fold these parcels as for omelette parcels [see p158–59].

1   Cut out and discard the thick stems at the base of each of the cabbage leaves. Bring a large pot of water to boil, and blanch the cabbage leaves for about 2 minutes. Remove and immerse immediately in a bowl of cold water. Pat any excess water off the leaves.

2   Mix the sushi rice with the herbs, scrambled eggs, and sesame seeds in a bowl.

3   Place a cabbage leaf on a clean surface or cutting board; put a tablespoonful of the rice mixture in the middle of it.

4   Fold over the near and far edges of the leaf so that they overlap in the middle. Then fold the other opposite edges over to make a parcel.

5   Secure the parcel by piercing it with a small wooden skewer or toothpick. Repeat the process to make 8 parcels. Be sure to remind guests to remove the skewers or toothpicks before eating.

Ingredients

8 large savoy cabbage leaves

½ quantity prepared sushi rice [p36–8]

½ cup mixed herbs such as flat leaf parsley, cilantro, scallion, or mint, finely chopped

1 quantity scrambled eggs [p43]

2 tbsp toasted sesame seeds

8 wooden skewers or toothpicks

Makes 8 parcels

Preparation time
45 minutes

Choose tender young cabbage for this fresh-tasting stuffed sushi.

Seared duck breast in rice paper parcels

Pan-fried duck breast is wrapped in Thai rice paper and drizzled with traditional Japanese teriyaki sauce in this innovative recipe. Teriyaki sauce can be bought already made but it's worth taking a little extra time to make this delicious version yourself. Serve it as a dipping sauce or keep it for up to a week in a sealed container in the refrigerator.

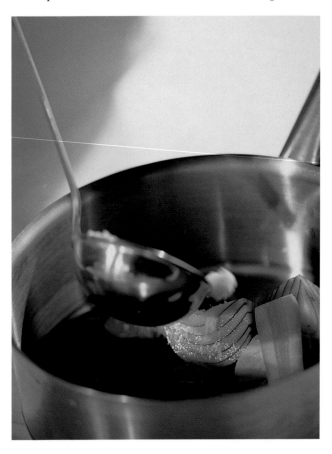

Ingredients

for savory teriyaki sauce:
2fl oz [60ml] mirin

2fl oz [60ml] soy sauce

2 tbsp sugar

2in [5cm] piece fresh
ginger, peeled

2in [5cm] piece
carrot, peeled

1 medium onion,
peeled and halved

for parcels:
1 duck breast

4 round sheets rice paper

½ quantity prepared
sushi rice [p36–8]

½ cucumber, cut
into thin strips

Makes 4 parcels

Preparation time
45 minutes

1 Put the ingredients for the teriyaki sauce in a small saucepan and heat gently. Stir until the sugar dissolves, then leave to simmer until the sauce has thickened to a syrupy consistency, about 20 minutes. Meanwhile prepare the duck.

2 Use a sharp knife to cut a series of shallow slits in the skin of the duck breast to help the fat drain away.

3 Heat a heavy-bottomed skillet over medium heat. Cook the duck breast skin-side-down until brown and crispy, about 5–10 minutes. Turn over and cook for 3–5 minutes more.

4 Remove the duck from the heat and plunge into a bowl of boiling water, or pour boiling water over to wash off excess fat. Remove from the water; set aside to cool to room temperature.

5 Fill a baking pan with warm water. Place the sheets of rice paper in it and soak until soft, about 2–3 minutes. Remove and drain on paper towel. Cut the duck into ¼ in [5mm] thick slices.

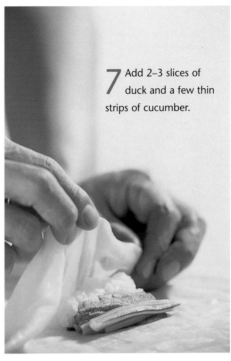

7 Add 2–3 slices of duck and a few thin strips of cucumber.

6 Spread the rice paper on a clean surface or cutting board. Put a large tablespoon of rice in the center and flatten slightly with the back of a spoon.

8 To wrap, bring the bottom edge of the rice paper over the filling, then fold in the sides. Continue to wrap to make a small parcel.

9 To serve, cut the parcel diagonally and arrange on a serving plate. Strain the teriyaki sauce and drizzle over the parcels.

Stuffed sushi inspired by Peking roast duck pancakes.

Pressed sushi
oshi zushi

This is the oldest form of sushi and probably developed from the ancient method of preserving fish by packing it tightly in boxes of fermented rice. Rice and other ingredients are pressed together in a wooden sushi mold to form a block, which is then cut into bite-sized pieces. Until the mid-19th century when hand-formed sushi, or *nigiri zushi*, was invented, all sushi was made in this way. Today, pressed sushi made with vinegar-marinated mackerel is the most popular take-out food bought at airports by Japanese travelers going abroad.

The recipes for pressed sushi that follow use a wooden pressed sushi mold [see p23], but a cake pan lined with plastic wrap makes a very good substitute. Of the many different types of sushi, pressed sushi is most suited to advance preparation. In fact, I prefer to make it up to six hours in advance – this allows time for the flavors of the sushi rice and topping to develop. Wrap each pressed block in plastic wrap and store at a cool, room temperature, then cut into small pieces to serve. Prepare a selection with different toppings, and serve them as elegant and delicious canapés.

< Use a knife dipped in vinegared water or wiped with a wet cloth to ensure clean cuts when slicing pressed sushi.

> Create designer sushi by arranging strips of ingredients in the bottom of the sushi mold to give a striped effect when turned out.

Pressed sushi
o s h i   z u s h i

All the pressed sushi recipes that follow use a rectangular mold that measures 6in [15cm] x 3in [7.5cm] x 2in [5cm]. Soak the mold in a bowl of water for about 15 minutes beforehand with a weight, such as a plate, on it to keep it from floating – this prevents the rice from sticking to it. You can prepare as far as step 7 up to six hours in advance.

Ingredients

1 marinated mackerel fillet [p92–3], about 5oz [150g]

wasabi

½ quantity prepared sushi rice [p36–8]

Makes 6 pieces

Preparation time
30 minutes

1 Trim the mackerel fillet so it is as thin and flat as possible. The excess can be used to fill gaps in the mold, so don't discard it.

2 Cut the fillet to fit the base of the mold, and lay it skin-side-down inside the box. Fill any gaps with smaller pieces of mackerel.

3 Cover the bottom of the mold with a patchwork of fillet cuts. Spread a few dabs of wasabi over the mackerel.

4 Add the sushi rice to the mold (it should be about two-thirds full), and use your fingers to pack it down evenly over the mackerel fillets.

5 Put the lid on the mold and press it down firmly to compact the rice.

6 With both thumbs on the lid of the mold, holding it in place, lift off the sides. Then take the lid off and carefully turn the mold over onto a cutting board, so the mackerel is on top.

7 Remove the base of the mold. If preparing in advance, wrap the block in plastic wrap and store in a cool place for up to 6 hours, but don't refrigerate.

8 Dip a sharp knife in water, wiping off the excess, and cut the block of sushi in half.

9 Cut each half into 3 equally sized pieces to make 6 pieces, and serve with pickled ginger.

Pressed mackerel sushi – excellent served with pickled ginger.

Soy-basted conger eel sushi

Conger eel or *anago* is available cooked and basted in soy, and either frozen or vacuum-packed from Japanese food stores. Try microwaving it for 20–30 seconds to revive its flavor before you use it in this sushi.

Follow the recipe for Pressed Sushi [see p170–73], but substitute the conger eel for the mackerel and omit the wasabi.

Ingredients

8 oz [250 g] soy-basted conger eel

½ quantity prepared sushi rice [p36–8]

Makes 6 pieces

Preparation time
20 minutes

Shrimp and nori sushi

Shrimp makes a good sushi ingredient for those who are wary of uncooked fish. Remember to lay the shrimp pink-side-down in the mold.

1   Open the shrimp flat and lay them pink-side-down on the bottom of the wet sushi mold, covering the entire bottom of the box. Dab a little wasabi on the shrimp, if using.
2   Fill the mold with half of the prepared sushi rice.
3   Cut a sheet of nori to fit the mold and gently press it down onto the rice.
4   Add the rest of the rice so the mold is nearly full. Put the lid on the mold, and press down gently.
5   Unmold the rice and shrimp block, and use a knife dipped in water to cut it into 6 equally sized pieces.

Ingredients

Approximately 12 medium shrimp, cooked, cleaned and butterflied [p110–11], tail shells removed

wasabi [optional]

½ quantity prepared sushi rice [p36–8]

2 sheets nori seaweed

Makes 6 pieces

Preparation time
20 minutes

Lunch box favorites, shrimp and nori, and conger eel pressed sushi.

Omelette and mustard sprout sushi

This simple recipe adds an exotic twist to the classic combination of egg and sprouts. If you cannot find mustard sprouts, use any similar leafy sprouts or watercress.

1 Line the base of a wet sushi mold with a layer of omelette. Fill the mold two-thirds full with sushi rice, put the lid on it, and press gently to compact the rice.
2 Unmold the rice and egg block, and use a knife dipped in water to cut it into 6 equally sized pieces.
3 Trim the root ends off the sprouts, and top each piece of sushi with a small peppery bunch of sprouts.

> ### Ingredients
> *2 thin Japanese omelettes [p44–5]*
> *½ quantity prepared sushi rice [p36–8]*
> *2 cartons mustard sprouts*
>
> **Makes 6 pieces**
>
> **Preparation time**
> 45 minutes

Asparagus and red pepper sushi

Here, the sushi mold is used to shape the rice, and the toppings are added later.

1 Grill the red pepper whole until the skin blackens. Put it in a bowl, cover with plastic wrap, and set aside to cool.
2 Meanwhile, steam or blanch the asparagus until tender, about 4 minutes, then plunge into a bowl of ice cold water.
3 Peel the skin off the red pepper and discard the seeds and the pith. Slice into thin strips.
4 Fill a wet sushi mold two-thirds full with sushi rice and put the lid on it. Press gently to compact the rice.
5 Unmold the block of rice, and use a knife dipped in water to cut it into 6 equally sized pieces.
6 Cut the asparagus stalks in half lengthwise and trim to the length of the rice blocks. Arrange them in a row on the rice and make a crisscross pattern on top with the red pepper.

> ### Ingredients
> *1 large red pepper*
> *12 small asparagus spears*
> *½ quantity prepared sushi rice [p36–8]*
>
> **Makes 6 pieces**
>
> **Preparation time**
> 40 minutes

Pressed sushi with multicolored toppings is always impressive.

Avocado and shiitake mushroom sushi

This recipe combines Eastern and Western ingredients in a simple and light sushi. The vinegar in the rice balances the high oil content of the avocado.

1   Line the base of a wet sushi mold with the avocado slices, then add the sushi rice. Put the lid on the mold, and press gently to compact the rice.
2   Unmold the rice and avocado block, and use a knife dipped in water to cut it into 6 equally sized pieces.
3   Top each piece of sushi with the shiitake mushroom slices.

Ingredients

1 ripe avocado, sliced

½ quantity prepared sushi rice [p36–8]

6 seasoned shiitake mushrooms [p31], sliced

Makes 6 pieces

Preparation time
30 minutes

Smoked salmon and cucumber sushi

The skill is in arranging the strips of salmon and cucumber. This sushi looks impressive but takes practice to perfect.

1   Trim the salmon and cucumber strips so that they fit the mold exactly when placed diagonally in it. Line the base of the wet sushi mold with alternating diagonal strips of smoked salmon and cucumber.
2   Add the sushi rice, then put the lid on the mold and press gently to compact it.
3   Unmold the rice, salmon, and cucumber block, and use a knife dipped in water to cut it into 6 equally sized pieces.

Ingredients

3½oz [100g] smoked salmon, cut into strips

6in [15cm] piece of cucumber, cut lengthwise into thin strips

½ quantity prepared sushi rice [p36–8]

Makes 6 pieces

Preparation time
30 minutes

Arrange toppings in stripes for a sophisticated effect.

Shiitake mushroom and zasai sushi

This Chinese-inspired sushi uses zasai, a pickled vegetable with dark green knobbly skin and a crunchy texture. Look for it in jars or cans in any Southeast Asian food shop.

1 Soak the zasai in water for about an hour, then drain and cut into thin slices.
2 Line the bottom of a wet sushi mold with the slices of zasai. Fill the mold half full with sushi rice.
3 Add a layer of shiitake mushroom slices. Put the lid on the mold, and press gently to compact the rice.
4 Unmold the zasai, mushroom, and rice block, and use a knife dipped in water to cut it into 6 equally sized pieces.

Ingredients

3½oz [100g] pickled zasai root

½ quantity prepared sushi rice [p36–8]

8 seasoned shiitake mushrooms [p31], sliced

Makes 6 pieces

Preparation time
30 minutes

Sea bass and perilla leaf sushi

The chile garnish gives a fiery boost to this delicate sushi. Try to cut the sea bass thinly enough for the green of the perilla leaf to show through the translucent fish.

1 Line the bottom of a wet sushi mold with a thin layer of sea bass. Add a thin layer of perilla leaves.
2 Add the sushi rice, put the lid on the mold and press gently to compact the rice.
3 Unmold the sea bass, perilla leaf, and rice block, and use a knife dipped in water to cut it into 6 equally sized pieces.
4 Garnish each piece of sushi with a couple of slices of chile.

Ingredients

3–4oz [90–120g] sea bass fillet, thinly sliced [p88–9]

½ quantity prepared sushi rice [p36–8]

about 10 perilla leaves

1 hot red chile, cut into thin rounds, to garnish

Makes 6 pieces

Preparation time
30 minutes

Sea bass and perilla sushi in front of shiitake mushroom and zasai sushi.

Children's sushi
kodomo zushi

There is no reason why children should be excluded from the pleasures of eating sushi. The most enthusiastic and obliging guinea pigs for testing my recipes have been my three children. Start with more familiar toppings such as ham, cheese, and smoked salmon, and use cookie cutters to create fun shapes; use the excess as garnishes.

1   Moisten the cookie cutters with water to prevent the rice from sticking to them. Use one third of the rice to make shapes in the first cookie cutter [see below]. Cut corresponding shapes out of the omelette and use as a topping. Repeat with the second third of rice in another cookie cutter and use smoked salmon as a topping. Make shapes with the remaining rice and sprinkle soboro on top of the rice.

2   Garnish each shape with cucumber, excess from the toppings, or with other smaller cut-out shapes.

Ingredients

1 quantity prepared sushi rice [p36–8]

1 thin Japanese omelette [p44–5]

1 oz [30g] thinly sliced smoked salmon

½ quantity soboro [p47]

cucumber to garnish

other suggested toppings that use ⅓ of the rice to make 8 pieces each:

½ quantity scrambled eggs [p43]

8 cheese slices

2 oz [60g] thinly sliced honey roasted ham

Makes about 24 pieces

Preparation time
45 minutes

Use the back of a teaspoon to compact the rice.

Hold the rice in place as you lift the cookie cutter.

Children's sushi can be as much fun to make as to eat.

Rolled sushi
maki zushi

The perfect party food or dinner party appetizer, rolled sushi is probably the most recognizable sushi. It consists of rice and fish, vegetables, or omelette rolled into a cylinder with nori seaweed around it and may also be called *nori maki*. There are many different types of rolled sushi: thin rolls, *hoso maki*, contain a single ingredient such as tuna or cucumber; thick rolls, *futo maki*, have several different fillings and combine a variety of flavors, colors, and textures; inside-out rolls, *uramaki*, have rice on the outside and nori on the inside; hand-rolled sushi, *temaki zushi*, are cone-shaped.

Once prepared, rolled sushi should be eaten right away since the nori quickly absorbs the moisture from the rice and becomes soggy. If left too long, the sushi rice expands and can split the nori. However, it is less important that the nori in the inside-out roll remains crisp so they can be prepared up to three hours in advance. Rolled sushi is not as difficult as hand-formed sushi and the Japanese often prepare it at home. With a little practice and a bamboo rolling mat, it's not difficult to achieve impressive results. As always, prepare your rice and other ingredients in advance.

< Once you've mastered the technique, experiment with combinations of fillings with different textures and colors for impressive effects.

> Hand-rolled sushi is party sushi and very easy to do; simply prepare platters of different fillings and let your guests roll their own.

Thin-roll sushi
h o s o   m a k i   z u s h i

This is believed to be the original form of rolled sushi and uses a single filling such as tuna, cucumber, or seasoned kampyo. Use whatever filling you prefer, but keep it simple. Once you have mastered thin-roll sushi, the other varieties are easy. This elegant bite-sized sushi makes wonderful finger food and is a guaranteed success as a dinner party appetizer.

1 Mix the ingredients for the vinegared water in a small bowl and set aside. Lay a sushi rolling mat on your work surface. Fold a sheet of nori in half across the grain, and pinch along the folded edge to break it in two. Place a halved sheet along the edge of the rolling mat with the shiny, smooth side facing down.

Ingredients

for vinegared water:
1–2 tbsp rice vinegar
8 fl oz [250 ml] water

for sushi rolls:
4–5 sheets nori seaweed

1 quantity prepared
sushi rice [p36–8]

wasabi paste

1 skinless fillet of tuna,
about 4 oz [125 g], cut into
pencil-thin strips [p89–91]

½ cucumber, cut into
½ in [1 cm] square strips

½ quantity thick Japanese
omelette [p40–42], cut into
½ in [1 cm] square strips

other suggested fillings that
make about 3 rolls each:

1 skinless fillet of salmon,
about 4 oz [125 g], cut into
pencil-thin strips [p89–91]

4 oz [125 g] crabmeat

1 medium carrot, cut into ½ in
[1 cm] square strips
and lightly steamed

Makes 8–10 rolls

Preparation time
45 minutes

2 Dip your hands in the vinegared water to prevent the rice from sticking to them. Take a handful of rice and form it into a log shape.

3 Place the rice in the center of the sheet of nori and use the tips of your fingers to spread it evenly over it. Leave about a ½ in [1cm] margin of nori along the edge furthest from you.

4 If using a fish filling, dab a thin line of wasabi paste across the center of the rice. Don't overdo the wasabi – it should compliment the flavor of the sushi, not overpower it.

5 Arrange a strip of tuna [or cucumber or omelette] on top of the wasabi. You may need to use two or three short pieces, but line them up close to each other with no gaps between them.

6 Lift up the edge of the mat closest to you, and slowly roll away from you in a smooth movement.

7 Roll the mat over so that the top edge of the nori meets the edge of the rice. You need to keep a gentle pressure on the roll to keep it neatly compacted.

8 You should be able to see the strip of nori not covered by rice. Gently shape the length of the roll using both hands and applying even pressure.

9 Lift the edge of the mat slightly and push the roll forward a little so that the uncovered strip of nori seals the roll. The moisture from the rice acts as an adhesive.

10 Push in any stray grains of rice to neaten the ends. Set aside in a cool place – but not the refrigerator – while you make more.

11 Dip a cloth or dish towel in the vinegared water, moisten a sharp knife, and cut each roll in half.

12 Moisten the knife with the cloth between each cutting. Place the two halves next to each other and cut them twice to make 6 equal bite-sized pieces. Arrange on a serving plate and serve immediately.

Simple and elegant thin-roll sushi with tuna, cucumber, and omelette.

Thick-roll sushi
f u t o   m a k i   z u s h i

Because of their colorful assortment of fillings, *futo maki* are also known as *date maki* or "dandy rolls." The rolling technique is similar to thin rolls, but these larger rolls use a whole sheet of nori instead of half of one. Experiment with different combinations of fillings to create colorful patterns, but be sure to prepare all the fillings before you start assembling the rolls. Eat these rolls immediately once prepared.

1 Mix the ingredients for the vinegared water in a small bowl and set aside. Lay a bamboo rolling mat on your work surface and place a sheet of nori shiny-side-down on it. Dip your hands in the vinegared water, form two handfuls of rice into log shapes and place at the center of the nori.

Ingredients

for vinegared water:
1–2 tbsp rice vinegar
8 fl oz [250 ml] water

3 sheets nori seaweed

1 quantity prepared
sushi rice [p36–8]

1 carrot, cut into
pencil-thin strips
and lightly steamed

1 oz [30g] green beans,
trimmed and lightly steamed

1 oz [30g] seasoned shiitake
mushrooms [p31]

1 thick Japanese omelette
[p40–42], cut into
½ in [1cm] strips

1 oz [30g] prepared
kampyo [p30]

other fillings that could
be substituted for any
of the above:

1 oz [30g] skinless fillet of fish
such as salmon, tuna, or red
snapper, cut into pencil-thin
strips [p89–91]

1 oz [30g] crabmeat
or lobster meat

1 oz [30g] spinach or avocado

3 seasoned tofu pouches [p46],
cut into ½ in [1cm] strips

Makes 3 rolls

Preparation time
45 minutes

2 Spread the rice evenly across the whole width of the nori, leaving a 1¾ in [4cm] margin on the edge of the nori furthest from you.

3 Lay one third of the carrot strips in the center of the rice with a third of the green beans and a third of the shiitake mushrooms on either side.

4 Arrange a third of the omelette strips and a third of the kampyo on either side of the green beans and shiitake mushrooms.

5 Place your thumbs under the rolling mat and lift the near edge of the mat with your thumbs and index fingers. Hold the fillings in place with the rest of your fingers.

6 Holding a small flap at the top of the mat, bring the near side of the roll over so that it covers the fillings.

7 Bring the rolling mat down to meet the strip of nori, and gently squeeze along the length of the roll to tuck in the near edge of the nori.

8 Lift the front edge of the mat slightly with one hand and use the other to gently push the roll forward so that the strip of nori not covered by rice seals the roll.

9 Pull back the mat and neaten the ends. Set aside in a cool place, but not the refrigerator, while you prepare the remaining 2 rolls. Use a knife moistened with vinegared water to cut the roll in half. Cut each half into six slices. When you get more confident you can place the 2 halves alongside each other and cut them together.

Slices of thick-roll sushi, or *futo maki*, always look impressive.

Inside-out roll sushi
uramaki

Despite appearances, this type of rolled sushi is easier
to prepare than the traditional nori-outside version.
The stickiness of the rice ensures that the sushi holds
together and is surprisingly rigid. Another advantage
of this type of sushi is that inside-out rolls can be
prepared in advance as it is less important for the nori
to stay crisp. The "California roll" demonstrated here
traditionally contains crab and avocado. It was first
created by an American-born Japanese chef in the
early 70s to overcome early squeamishness about
eating raw fish – it has since become a classic.

Ingredients

for vinegared water:
*2–3 tbsp rice vinegar
8fl oz [250ml] water*

3 sheets nori seaweed

for sushi rolls:
*1 quantity prepared
sushi rice [p36]*

4oz [120g] crabmeat [p98]

*1 baby cucumber
[or ¼ of a large one],
cut into pencil-thin strips*

12 tsps mayonnaise,

wasabi paste, if desired

*1 medium avocado,
halved and pitted, sliced
lengthwise into thin strips*

6 tbsp flying fish roe

Makes 6 rolls

Preparation time
35 minutes

1 Mix the ingredients for
the vinegared water in
a small bowl and set aside.
Lay a bamboo rolling mat
on your work surface, and
cover it with plastic wrap.

2 Break a nori sheet in half [see step 1, p186] and place it on the mat. Dip your hands in the vinegared water, take a handful of rice and place it in the middle of the nori. Use your fingers to spread an even layer of rice to the edges of the nori. Pick up the rice-covered nori and quickly turn it over on the mat.

3 Lay the crab and cucumber along the center of the nori. Add a line of mayonnaise alongside, and a thin smear of wasabi, if using. Arrange a layer of avocado on top.

4 Lift up the near edge of the mat, holding the fillings in place with your fingers, if necessary. Start rolling to join the 2 edges of the rice and nori sheet together.

5 Gently squeeze along the length of the roll to mold it together, then lift up the front edge of the mat and push the roll forward to join the 2 edges of nori. Use gentle but firm pressure to shape the log into a round or square shape.

6 Open the mat. Spoon the fish roe onto the sushi roll, and use the back of a spoon to spread the roe over it. Turn the roll over to coat the underside. The roe does not have to cover the sushi perfectly.

7 Dip a cloth or dish towel in the vinegared water, moisten a sharp knife, and cut each roll in half. Place the 2 halves next to each other, moisten the knife, and cut twice for 6 equally sized pieces.

Flying fish roe adds a touch of vibrant orange to inside-out rolls.

Log-roll sushi
bō zushi

This simple but delicious rolled sushi uses vinegar-marinated mackerel as a wrapping material instead of nori. It is an excellent way to enjoy the taste of marinated mackerel if you don't have a pressed sushi mold. Be sure to leave adequate time to prepare the fish, and let the roll stand for 30 minutes at room temperature before cutting to allow time for the flavors to develop.

Ingredients

for vinegared water:
2–3 tbsp rice vinegar
8 floz [250ml] water

½ quantity prepared
sushi rice [p36–8]

2 vinegar-marinated
mackerel fillets [p92],
about 5oz [150g] each

wasabi paste [optional]

Makes 2 rolls

Preparation time
45 minutes

1 Mix the ingredients for the vinegared water in a small bowl and set aside. Lay a rolling mat on your work surface and cover both sides of it in plastic wrap.

2 Wet your hands with vinegared water. Place two small handfuls of rice in the center of the rolling mat and shape into a mackerel-length log.

3 Dab the underside of the mackerel with a little wasabi, if using. Place the fillet on top of the mound of rice, skin-side up.

4 Lift the mat over the rice and mackerel so that it is completely covered.

5 Work your hands along the length of the sushi log, squeezing it firmly but gently. If the mackerel is longer than the rice, neaten it by pressing the ends of the fish over so that they stick to the rice.

6 Set aside to stand for 20 minutes at room temperature. Dip a cloth or dish towel in the vinegared water and moisten a sharp knife. Slice the log into bite-sized pieces.

Easy to make, beautiful to look at, and quick to eat – log-roll sushi.

Hand-rolled sushi
temaki zushi

This sushi makes a perfect dinner party appetizer and involves very little effort on the host's part. Simply prepare the sushi rice and cut up a colorful selection of fillings, then let your guests roll their own sushi. Use 3½ oz [100g] of skinless fish fillet per person as a rough guide [try to use at least two kinds of fish], but err on the generous side rather than risk running out.

Ingredients

10 sheets nori seaweed, halved [p186]

1 quantity prepared sushi rice [p36–8]

wasabi paste

your choice of fillings such as:

14oz [400g] fish in total, cut for hand-rolled sushi [p88–91] any of:
sea bass or red snapper;
tuna or salmon;
turbot, brill, or lemon sole;
vinegar-marinated mackerel or smoked salmon

3½oz [100g] salmon roe or flying fish roe

½ quantity thick Japanese omelette [p40–42]

14oz [400g] vegetables in total, cut into pencil-thin strips 2¾in [6cm] long, any of:
avocado, pitted;
cucumber;
fresh carrot;
pickled daikon;
green beans, trimmed and blanched;
1 carton mustard sprouts;
10 perilla leaves

Makes 20 cones

Preparation time
45 minutes

1 Hold a piece of nori in your left hand, and put a generous tablespoon of rice in the top left-hand corner.

2 Spread the rice to the
center of the bottom edge
of the nori. Use your finger to
flatten the rice slightly, then
dab a little wasabi paste on it.

3 Arrange your choice of
fillings on top of the rice
so they point diagonally to the
top left corner of the nori.

4 Fold the bottom left-hand corner of the nori toward the top right-hand corner, wrapping it around the rice and fillings.

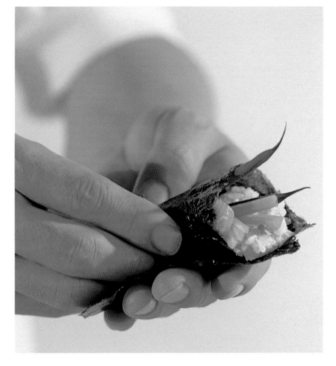

5 Continue rolling until the nori forms a cone shape that holds the rice and fillings.

Create your own combinations with hand-rolled sushi.

Hand-formed sushi
nigiri zushi

A relatively new addition to the sushi repertoire, *nigiri zushi* is less than 200 years old. It was first invented as a street food in the old capital Edo, now Tokyo, and totally revolutionized sushi because it took so little time to make. *Nigiri* means "to squeeze" – when a sushi chef makes *nigiri zushi*, he gently squeezes a small quantity of rice into an oval, adds a perfectly judged amount of wasabi paste, then presses on a topping, usually of fish. But there is more to it than simply making balls of rice and putting slices of fish on top. The perfect piece of *nigiri zushi* should be the right size to eat in one mouthful and the rice should gently fall apart on your tongue, not in your fingers or chopsticks. The gentle tartness of the sushi rice should complement the topping, not compete with it, and a hint of wasabi should enhance the flavor.

Start with Easy Hand-Formed Sushi [see p214–17], and progress to the expert's method when you have perfected the technique. While the rice is cooking, prepare the toppings. Have a bowl of vinegared water nearby to dip your fingers in from time to time to prevent the rice from sticking to them, then begin the assembly.

< *Nigiri zushi* is the most popular type of sushi and is what many people think of when the word sushi is mentioned.

> Toppings have changed with the times: abalone, sea bream, and flounder were traditional; tuna and mackerel only became popular after World War II.

Expert hand-formed sushi
nigiri zushi

This is the ultimate sushi. It looks deceptively simple when prepared by a sushi chef, but is in fact one of the most difficult. A sushi master spends years perfecting his technique and produces each piece of sushi in what appears to be one smooth movement taking only a matter of seconds. In his expert hands the pieces tend to be marginally smaller than Easy Hand-Formed Sushi [see p214–7], and use less rice but slightly more fish.

Ingredients

*1 quantity prepared
sushi rice [p36–8]*

*1lb [500g] skinless fillet of
any fish such as red snapper,
salmon, tuna, sole, brill,
or sea bass, cut for hand-
formed sushi [p88–91]*

wasabi paste

Makes 40–50 pieces

---

1 Mix 8fl oz [250ml] water
and 2–3 tbsp vinegar in
a small bowl and wet hands
in it to prevent the rice from
sticking to them.

2 Take a small handful of rice in your
right hand and gently mold it into
a rounded oblong.

3 Holding the ball of rice loosely in your right fist, pick up the topping with your left hand. Lay the topping across your fingers, and dab a little wasabi paste on it.

4 Hold the rice between your right thumb and index finger, and gently press it onto the topping with your left thumb.

5 Hold the sushi halfway along its sides, between your thumb and index finger. Spin the sushi 180° so the topping is on top.

6 Squeeze the sides of the sushi between your right forefinger and thumb to shape it and compact the rice.

7 Cup the sushi in your left hand and use two fingers to press gently on the top to compact it more.

8 Open your left hand and spin the sushi around, keeping the topping on top. Repeat steps 6 and 7 to shape the sushi.

Red snapper makes a delicate topping for *nigiri zushi*.

Easy hand-formed sushi
nigiri zushi

Nigiri zushi is the most difficult sushi to master – even the Japanese rarely make it at home. This is an easier – and quicker – basic method of preparation. The results are really the same, although a sushi master might disagree. Use 3½oz [100g] fish per person, which makes five pieces, as a rough guide. As with the expert's version, prepare your toppings beforehand.

Ingredients

for vinegared water:
2–3 tbsp rice vinegar
8 floz [250ml] water

for hand-formed sushi:
1 quantity prepared
sushi rice [p36–8]

14 oz [400g] fish preferably
several different types
[p52–129], cut for
hand-formed sushi [p88]

wasabi paste

½ quantity thick Japanese
omelette [40–42], cut into
slices ¼in [0.5cm] thick

5 strips nori seaweed
½in [1cm] x 3in [7.5cm] for
tying the omelette topping

Makes 24–32 pieces

Preparation time
45 minutes

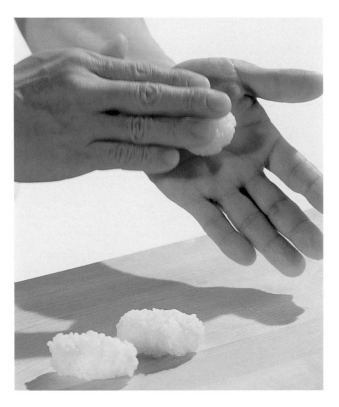

1 Mix the ingredients for the vinegared water in a small bowl. Dip your hands in the mixture and pick up a ball of rice about the size of an egg. Gently roll it in the palm of your hands, shaping it into an oblong. Place it on a clean work surface or cutting board. Prepare several at a time.

2 Neaten the shape of the rice balls, if necessary, but don't over-handle the rice.

3 Lay the toppings out next to each oblong of rice. Dab a little wasabi paste on each oblong of rice. Omit wasabi if using omelette as a topping.

4 Lay the topping on each rice oblong, and press gently to keep it in place. Avoid excessive handling of the fish.

5 If using fish as a topping, use your thumb and forefinger to press the ends of the fish to the rice.

6 Gently shape the sides of the rice. If using omelette as a topping, tie the sushi with a strip of nori.

Sushi with tuna, sea bass, salmon, marinated mackerel, and omelette.

Battleship sushi
gunkan maki

Sushi toppings such as fish roe and oysters simply will not stay on the sushi rice without some form of containment. This type of sushi is called *gunkan maki* because the strip of nori seaweed that keeps the topping in place gives it a battleship shape. The nori absorbs the moisture from the rice and the topping and becomes soggy if left too long, so make this type of sushi last if you are making a selection.

Ingredients

for vinegared water:
2–3 tbsp rice vinegar
8 fl oz [250 ml] water

for sushi:
3 sheets nori seaweed,
each cut into 6 equal strips

½ quantity prepared
sushi rice [p36–8]

wasabi paste

4 oz [120 g] of flying fish roe,
[can be dyed red, green, or
natural colored]

6 oysters

2 oz [60 g] salmon roe

Makes 18 pieces

Preparation time
30 minutes

1 Mix the ingredients for the vinegared water in a small bowl and set aside. Put 2 sheets of nori on top of each other, and cut into 6 equal-sized strips about 1 in [2½ cm] wide and 6 in [15 cm] long.

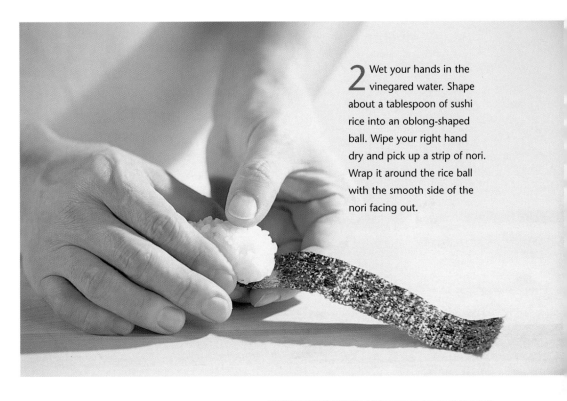

2 Wet your hands in the vinegared water. Shape about a tablespoon of sushi rice into an oblong-shaped ball. Wipe your right hand dry and pick up a strip of nori. Wrap it around the rice ball with the smooth side of the nori facing out.

3 Crush a grain of cooked rice at the end of the strip of nori so that it sticks the nori down where it overlaps, to form a ring around the rice.

4 Dab a little wasabi paste on the rice and flatten the rice slightly.

5 Spoon the topping onto the rice, keeping it inside the ring of nori.

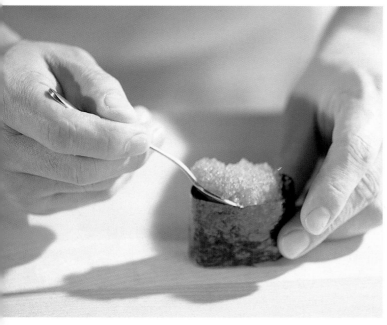

Dyed flying fish roes, salmon roe, oyster, and natural flying fish roe.

Plastic wrap sushi
temari zushi

This is one of the easiest types of sushi to make and you don't need any special equipment – just plastic wrap. Prepare these pretty canapés up to a day in advance, and keep them wrapped in plastic wrap until needed.

1 Divide the rice in half. Lay a piece of plastic wrap, about 4in [10cm] square, on a clean work surface and place a piece of smoked salmon at the center of it. Mold a teaspoonful of sushi rice into a loose ball and place on top of it.

2 Pick up all four corners of the plastic wrap and gather them in the middle. Twist the plastic wrap to compact the rice and form a small ball. Repeat the process to make 10 smoked salmon balls. Make 10 shrimp balls in the same way, but put half a teaspoonful of caviar in the crescent of each shrimp.

3 Keep each piece of sushi wrapped in the plastic wrap until just before serving. Put a dab of wasabi on each of the smoked salmon balls just before serving.

Ingredients

½ quantity prepared sushi rice [p36–8]

1oz [30g] smoked salmon, cut into 10 postage-stamp-size pieces

wasabi

10 cooked shrimp

1oz [30g] flying fish roe

other toppings that use the same quantity of rice to make 10 pieces each:

½ cucumber, sliced wafer thin and cut into postage-stamp-size pieces

1oz [30g] any variety of caviar

1oz [30g] rare roast beef, thinly sliced and cut into postage-stamp-size pieces

wasabi paste

Makes 20–30 pieces

Preparation time
25 minutes

Form the rice into a loose ball, but don't overhandle it.

Adjust the shape of the ball with your fingers, if necessary.

Smoked salmon with wasabi, and prawn and fish roe sushi balls.

Eating

At a sushi bar
a unique experience

Whether you have discovered sushi already or are just trying it for the first time, there is something very special about a visit to a sushi bar – you receive highly personalized service and almost all the food you eat is prepared in front of you. Marvel at the sushi chef's expertise, and rely on him for guidance – he will look after you.

Inside the sushi bar

Sushi bars tend to be small, intimate places and although interiors may vary, you will usually find a long, spotlessly clean counter with a refrigerated glass case behind it where the day's carefully prepared fish, shellfish, and roe are beautifully displayed. The master sushi chef stands behind the counter.

Most sushi bars will not accept reservations at the counter, which tends to operate on a first-come-first-served basis, since some customers will pop in for a quick snack while others will linger for the whole evening. You can usually reserve a table in a large restaurant.

Never feel intimidated or awkward – the goal of a good sushi bar is to provide excellent food and service in a relaxed atmosphere. The sushi master chef prides himself on maintaining the highest level of service possible.

< The sushi chef can cast his trained eye over the entire place from his position behind the counter.

> Order individual pieces of sushi or try a combination set, a good introduction to sushi.

No menu

Sushi bars are unique in that often there is no real menu – you order the toppings of your choice by simply pointing at the fish in the display case in front of you. In Japan, sushi bars often don't display prices because fresh fish is bought daily and prices inevitably fluctuate. As a result, there may be some uncertainty over your final bill, but if you feel uncomfortable about this, opt for a combination set. This usually consists of a selection of hand-formed and rolled sushi, or *nigiri zushi* and *maki zushi*, for a fixed, normally more reasonable, price. You can always order individual pieces in addition to the set.

The bill

A professional, trained sushi chef may be given written orders by waiters if the sushi bar is part of a restaurant, but he very rarely writes anything down. Instead, he keeps track of each customer's order, for as many as six people at a time, and discreetly adds up the total in his head when he is asked for the bill.

Tipping

The sushi chef takes pride in performing his craft and would not dream of asking for a tip. A gracious way of thanking him is to offer him a sake or a beer. If he accepts, order it from the waiter. The sushi chef will raise a toast to thank you, and you should drink to the good sushi you had with him. Outside Japan, unless a service charge is included, standard gratuity is customary.

Etiquette
dos and don'ts

There is something about the formal and orderly atmosphere of the sushi bar that can make even the most beautifully mannered non-Japanese diner feel awkward. Sushi bars are intimate but relaxed places without strict rules of conduct. Feeling at ease with the etiquette will not only help you relax, it will enhance your enjoyment of the meal.

Structuring the meal

The absence of a menu means that there is no obvious guidance on how to structure your meal. There is no correct order in which to eat sushi, though a sushi connoisseur might disagree.

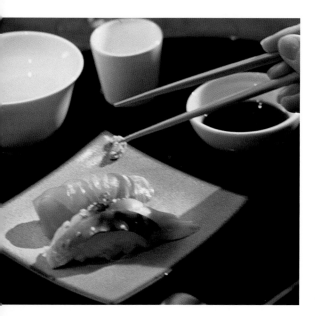

Choose whatever strikes your fancy and consider these conventional guidelines, but don't regard them as gospel.

• A few slices of sashimi can be a gentle start to a sushi meal – ask the sushi chef what he recommends.

• If you want to taste the sushi bar's vinegar mixture – a fair indication of the chef's skills – start with omelette topping – its subtle flavor allows you to taste the rice. However, I have also known sushi gurus to end a meal with omelette, treating it more like a sweet dessert.

• Start with blander tasting white fish and work your way toward richer fish with red meat and more strongly flavored toppings. A logical enough approach, but if your favorite topping is fatty belly of tuna, start with that.

• Some say that you should finish a meal with rolled sushi. This may be because

Chopstick etiquette

In a sushi bar, you are given a pair of disposable wooden chopsticks in a paper sleeve when you take your seat. Take the chopsticks out of the sleeve, break them apart, and rest them on the small chopstick rest in front of you.

• Don't pass food from your chopsticks to another person's chopsticks since this is considered to be extremely bad luck. In the traditional Japanese funeral ceremony, relatives pass the cremated bones of the deceased with chopsticks before collecting them in a burial pot.

• If you are helping yourself to food from a communal plate or serving someone else, it is polite to turn your chopsticks around and use the top ends.

they contain more rice and are therefore more filling than hand-formed sushi, but I don't think you should have to wait.

Fingers or chopsticks?

If you don't feel comfortable using chopsticks, it is perfectly acceptable to use your fingers [see p230]. Remember that hand-formed sushi was originally invented as a snack to be eaten at a street stand. You should be given a wet towel at the start of a meal at a sushi bar, so wipe your fingers on this before you begin.

The correct use of soy sauce

One of the most wonderful seasonings, soy sauce appears in almost every aspect of Japanese cooking. I love it and use it all the time, but for sushi, it should be used sparingly – for dipping and not for drowning the food.

There is an art to dipping a piece of hand-formed sushi into soy sauce without it disintegrating and leaving grains of rice floating in the dish. Whether you are using chopsticks or your fingers [see below], try to eat hand-formed sushi in one mouthful; it is considered impolite to bite a piece of sushi in half and then put the remaining half back on your plate.

When dipping a piece of rolled sushi, dip only a small corner of it in the soy sauce. Don't submerge the sushi – not only will it fall apart, but the rice will quickly absorb all the soy sauce and the delicate flavors of the roll will be totally overwhelmed.

The same technique applies for dipping battleship sushi in soy sauce.

how to dip your sushi

1 Pour a little soy sauce into a small dipping bowl. Pick up the piece of sushi, holding it between your thumb and middle finger.

2 Twist your hand slightly to dip the topping in the soy sauce. Pop it into your mouth upside-down, so you taste the topping first.

∧ **Pickled ginger**

Sushi is served with a little heap of thinly sliced pink, pickled ginger. It is intended as a palate cleanser and should be eaten a slice at a time in-between different types of sushi. Its refreshing flavor can make it rather addictive for some, but it is an accompaniment to sushi or sashimi, not a side salad, even though the sushi chef will happily keep replenishing it.

> **Wasabi**

I have watched people dissolve an entire mound of wasabi paste in their soy sauce dipping dish and then proceed to drown a piece of sushi or sashimi in it. Up until now I have recommended that you eat according to your personal tastes and not be intimidated by convention, but this is where I draw the line. Wasabi is an essential accompaniment to sushi and sashimi, but it is intended to enhance the flavor of the food and should never be regarded as a proof of bravery.

At a sushi bar, if you like the taste and sensation of wasabi, ask the chef to apply a little more to your sushi and he will be more than happy to oblige. If you are eating sashimi, dab a little wasabi paste on an individual slice and then dip it briefly in the soy sauce. This way, you can savor the unique flavor of the fish and yet still enjoy the essence of the wasabi and soy sauce.

What to drink
tea, beer, sake, and wine

Good sushi restaurants and bars offer a wide range of beverages, and the Japanese drink whatever they wish with their meal. The most traditional drinks in a sushi bar are probably hot green tea or sake – Japanese rice wine – but Japanese beer is also available. Sushi has become such an international food that both red and white wine are also popular choices.

Green tea

A cup of hot green tea, called *agari* in sushi bars, is not only refreshing but cleanses the palate during a sushi meal. It is a gentle digestive aid and contains vitamins A, B, and C.

Beer

There are three main breweries in Japan, but good sushi bars usually stock many different Japanese and non-Japanese beers – *birru*. Japanese beers tend to be closer in flavor to American and European lagers and are always served cold. Beer has a crisp, refreshing quality that goes well with sushi and sashimi.

Sake

The subtle flavor of sake enhances almost all Japanese food. It is quite potent, with an alcohol content of about

17 percent. Sake should be drunk at room temperature or even slightly chilled. You may, however, be served hot sake in a small bottle with a tiny cup. The practice of serving sake hot dates back to the post-war period when food scarcity meant that sake had to be made artificially and it was heated to disguise the inferior smell and flavor.

It is pleasant to drink warm sake in the winter – some say that the heat makes it more potent – and there are plenty of diehards who insist on heating it regardless of the time of year.

The Japanese rediscovered sake during the economic prosperity of the 80s and many small local brands have since become available even outside Japan. Sake comes in three grades: *tokkyu*, premium class, is the best and the most expensive; *ikkyu*, first class, is still excellent and *nikyu*, second class, is a perfectly drinkable table wine grade. However, the grading system gives no indication of the flavor, which can range from dry to sweet. The grading is only for the purposes of the tax system.

Wine

Any good Japanese restaurant or sushi bar should have a respectable wine list, and I often serve wine with sushi at home. I would always recommend that you drink whatever wine you like to drink, but for those who want to choose a wine depending on the topping or filling, here are some guidelines:

For vegetables, egg, or white fish, choose a full-bodied white wine such as a Burgundy, a crisp Sauvignon Blanc, or a ripe Chardonnay. For more robustly flavored vegetables such as mushrooms, try a light- or medium-bodied red such as a Pinot Noir or Chianti Classico, or a dry white wine such as a Reisling.

For shellfish such as tiger shrimp or crab, try champagne or sparkling white wine.

For strongly flavored fish such as tuna, salmon, or marinated mackerel, choose a medium- to full-bodied white such as a Burgundy or Chardonnay, or even a full-bodied red such as a Gamay.

Sushi at home
entertaining

Sushi is such an artistic and yet delicious food that it never fails to impress. Start simple, with scattered sushi for example, and progress to more challenging types as your sushi-making skills improve. Remember that hand-formed sushi requires a little more expertise, so if you want to impress your guests at a dinner party, try to have a practice-run first.

Entertaining at home

Provide chopsticks, a chopstick holder, and a small dipping bowl at each place setting. Offer wasabi and pickled ginger in communal bowls or arrange small mounds of each on a serving plate for people to help themselves. Put soy sauce on the table in a small jug.

Easy lunch menu Make a large dish of any scattered sushi [see p132–45] except Tokyo-style Sushi – this should be offered in individual bowls.

Easy dinner menu Start with Spring Miso Soup [see p238], then as a main course, provide a platter with a selection of fillings for Hand-Rolled Sushi [see p204–7]. What could be simpler than letting your guests roll their own sushi?

Easy vegetarian menu Start with Inside-Out Roll Sushi [see p196–9] substituting strips of cucumber and toasted sesame seeds for the crab and flying fish roe. Follow with Asparagus and Scrambled Egg Sushi, Snow Peas and Vine-Ripened Tomato Sushi [see p140–41] or any other vegetarian scattered sushi.

A light spring or summer menu
Prepare individual plates of sashimi [see p240–43]. Follow with rolled sushi made with three to five different fillings or toppings [see p184–203].

A warming fall or winter menu
Begin with a hot soup such as Clear Soup with White Fish [see p236–7], then follow with a plate of two to four different types of pressed sushi [see p168–83] or with indvidual bowls of Tokyo-style Sushi [see p134–7].

What to serve with sushi
The Japanese often serve soup at both ends of the meal. Traditionally, *sui mono*, which is similar to a sophisticated consommé, is served at the start. *Miso shiru*, or miso soup, served with a bowl of rice and a small dish of pickles usually signifies the end of the meal [see pages 236–39 for soups].

Sashimi makes a perfect appetizer for a sushi meal, typically accompanied by soy sauce, wasabi, pickled ginger, and shredded daikon [see p240–43].

Finish the meal with a selection of refreshing fresh fruit, sliced attractively.

Clear soup with egg and shiitake mushrooms

The egg in this soup separates into strands and provides a soft, delicate contrast to the earthy flavor of the shiitake mushrooms. Try to be artistic as you ladle it into bowls.

1 Heat the dashi stock in a small saucepan until it just boils, then remove from the heat.
2 Add the beaten egg, pouring it through a wire sieve to create strands. Use a whisk to make gentle waves in the pan to separate the strands. Don't whisk the soup.
3 Add the mushroom caps, and season with soy sauce, sake, and salt to taste. Bring back to a boil over a low heat, then immediately remove from the heat.
4 Ladle the soup into serving bowls, garnish with whole cilantro leaves, and serve.

Ingredients

1 quantity dashi stock [p39]

2 eggs, beaten

4 fresh shiitake mushrooms, stems removed

1 tbsp light soy sauce

1 tbsp sake

fresh cilantro to garnish

salt

Serves 4

Preparation time
25 minutes

Clear soup with white fish

Use any white fish such as red snapper, sole, or sea bass for this soup. Leaving the skin on the fish helps to keep its shape and also adds a decorative touch.

1 Bring the dashi stock to a boil in a small saucepan. Add the soy sauce, mirin, and salt to taste. Reduce the heat and simmer gently.
2 Add the fish to the pan and bring back to a boil, then immediately remove from the heat.
3 Put two pieces of fish skin-side-up in each individual bowl.
4 Gently ladle the soup over the fish, garnish with the sliced scallions, and serve.

Ingredients

1 quantity dashi stock [p39]

1 tbsp light soy sauce

1 tbsp mirin

4oz [125g] white fish fillets such as red snapper, sole, or sea bass, cut into 8 pieces

4 scallions, finely sliced

salt

Serves 4

Preparation time
20 minutes

Soup can be served either at the beginning or the end of the meal.

Clam miso soup
asari miso shiru

This classic miso soup is easy to prepare since the cooking water is used for the broth. The color of miso paste ranges from light cream to dark brown, but generally the darker it is, the saltier it tastes.

1   Dissolve the miso paste in a little hot water and add to a saucepan with the dashi stock and clams. Bring gently to a boil, skimming any residue from the surface, then remove from the heat.

2   Leave the lid on the saucepan for 1–2 minutes or until the clams have opened; discard any clams that do not open. Season the soup with salt to taste.

3   Ladle the soup into individual bowls, garnish with the sliced scallion, and serve.

Ingredients

4 tbsp miso paste

1 quantity dashi stock [p39]

20 clams, washed thoroughly [p126]

2 scallions, finely sliced

salt

Serves 4

Preparation time
20 minutes

Spring miso soup

I use purple broccoli in this soup, but you could substitute snow peas or asparagus. Use light miso paste – it won't overwhelm the delicate flavor of the vegetables.

1   Dissolve the miso paste in a little hot water and add to a saucepan with the dashi stock and broccoli. Bring to a boil over a gentle heat, then reduce the heat and simmer for 3 minutes. Season with salt to taste.

2   Add the cubed tofu and bring back to a boil, then remove from the heat.

4   Ladle the soup into individual bowls, garnish with the toasted sesame seeds, if using, and serve.

Ingredients

4 tbsp light miso paste

1 quantity dashi stock [p39]

8oz [250g] purple broccoli or rapini, tough stems removed

2oz [60g] firm tofu, cut into ½ in [1cm] cubes

1 tbsp toasted sesame seeds to garnish [optional]

salt

Serves 4

Preparation time
20 minutes

Spring miso soup with tofu in front of clam miso soup.

Sashimi
an introduction

To some, sashimi looks like sushi without the rice, but there is more
to it than sliced raw fish. Sashimi is one of the oldest Japanese cuisines
and has a history all its own. It may be incomprehensible to some, but
the Japanese believe that in most cases the less a food is cooked the
better, and the best way to cook a fish is to not cook it at all.

The origins of sashimi

In 123 AD the reigning Emperor was
served raw bonito and clams with
vinegar by his head chef – this was
sashimi in its earliest form. By the
middle of the 15th century, it was
recognized as a dish in its own right.

Known as *namasu*, it was eaten with
seasoned vinegar, not with soy sauce
as it is today. By the mid-17th century,
sea bass, red snapper, bonito, shark, eel,
perch, carp, shellfish, pheasant, and duck
were all used for sashimi. Many of these
were eaten raw but some were blanched
or lightly cooked. At around the same
time, soy sauce became widely available
and sashimi, in the form that we know
today, became popular.

Today, sashimi is regarded as the
perfect start to a Japanese meal. It is
served with soy sauce, wasabi, shredded
daikon, and sometimes fresh seaweed and
perilla leaves – accompaniments chosen
not just for their colors and flavors but
for their ability to aid digestion.

< Begin a sushi meal with a few slices
of sashimi – fish in its purest form.

Arranging a sashimi plate
and making garnishes

Generally, any fish that is suitable for sushi can also be used for sashimi. The most crucial factor is freshness, even more so than for sushi, since with sashimi there are no other ingredients to disguise the fish's flavor. Fish with red meat such as tuna, bonito, and mackerel are cut into thick slices, and white fish such as snapper, sole, and sea bass are sliced thinly since they tend to be firmer in texture [see p88–91]. Choose fish with both red and white meat for an arrangement, and decorate the plate with a few carefully chosen garnishes. Estimate about 4oz [125g] fish per person.

Garnishes

thin slices of lemon or lime

wasabi leaves [p51]

perilla leaves

shredded daikon [p49]

shrimp fantails [see below]

white fish roses [p242]

flying fish roe

prawn fantails

A specialty Japanese fishseller will sell raw shrimp glazed in a sugar and vinegar syrup. Make a shrimp fantail by laying a shrimp on its side on a cutting board. Hold it by its tail and and twist so that the body coils around the tail. Separate the individual shell pieces in the tail to make a decorative fan.

making a white fish rose

1 Use a 3in [7.5cm] wide fillet of white fish [about 4oz or 120g] such as red snapper, sole, or sea bass. Slice at a 45° angle and cut 3–4 thin strips as for hand-formed sushi [see p88–91]. Lay them in a line with each strip overlapping by about 1in [2.5cm]. This amount of fish will make four roses.

2 Roll up the line of fish strips. Use chopsticks, if necessary, to pick up the ends of each strip and to roll.

3 Set the rose on its base, and use chopsticks or your fingers to gently shape the "petals."

A skillfully arranged sashimi plate is an edible work of art.

Troubleshooting
problems and solutions

It takes years of practice and hard work to become a full-fledged sushi chef so don't be disappointed if you can't produce to sushi bar standards at first. If your initial attempts aren't perfect, in most cases they will still be salvageable. Here are solutions to some of the more common problems that you might encounter in your early days of sushi-making.

Scattered sushi
Problem The rice has solidified and it is difficult to mix in other ingredients.
Solution The rice may have become too cold. Sprinkle a tablespoonful of Japanese rice vinegar over it, then fold in gently to separate the grains. Always allow the rice to cool once prepared, but never refrigerate it since this will cause it to harden. Mix in other ingredients when the rice is room temperature.

Stuffed sushi
Problem The rice has solidified and become unmanageable.
Solution See Scattered sushi [left].
Problem The wrapping material has torn.
Solution You may have overstuffed the sushi. Continue to wrap or stuff as best you can, and serve with the torn part underneath so it is concealed. "What the eyes do not see, the heart will not grieve." If it is really torn, you may have to take out some filling and start over.

< Mix other ingredients into the rice when it is room temperature, otherwise it may solidify.

∧ Soak the sushi mold in cold water beforehand to prevent rice from sticking.

Pressed sushi

Problem The block of sushi is stuck in the pressed sushi mold.

Solution You may not have soaked the sushi mold in cold water for long enough beforehand [see p23]. Wet a butter knife with water and cut around the edges of the block to unstick the rice. When the block is free, neaten the edges with the wet knife.

Rolled sushi

Problem The filling is off-center.

Solution You may have positioned the filling incorrectly before rolling. Cut the roll into bite-sized pieces and use your fingers to try to recenter the fillings individually. If this does not work,

gently shape each piece into a tear drop shape with the filling at the narrow end. To serve, arrange the pieces of sushi in a circle with the fillings toward the center to make a sushi flower.

Problem The nori has split.

Solution You may have overfilled the roll with rice or with fillings. Place another sheet of nori seaweed on the rolling mat, put the roll split-side-down on it and re-roll it. Although the roll has double layers of nori, the moisture from the rice will meld them together. Alternatively, turn it into an inside-out roll [see p196–99].

∨ Don't fill rolled sushi with too many ingredients, otherwise the nori may split.

鮨 Glossary
useful japanese terms

Abura age	Puffy, brown deep-fried tofu [p46, 152]
Agari	Green tea served in sushi bars
Aji	Spanish or horse mackerel [p54]
Akami	Lean tuna, cut from the back of the fish [p60]
Aka gai	Ark shell clam [p126]
Ama ebi	Sweet shrimp, usually served raw [p108]
Anago	Conger eel [p128, 174], served basted in a sweet soy sauce
Asari	Common clam [p126]
Awabi	Abalone [p118]
Baka gai	Round clam [p126]
Battera	Pressed mackerel sushi [p62, 170]
Birru	Beer
Bō zushi	Log-roll sushi [p200]
Chakin zushi	"Stuffed purse" sushi [p160]
Chirashi zushi	Scattered sushi [p132]
Chu toro	Medium fatty tuna, from the upper belly [p61]
Daikon	Long white radish [p33] also known as a mouli
Dashi	Basic fish stock [p39]
Dashi maki tamago	Thick, sweet omelette [p40]
Deba bōchō	Type of knife – cleaver [p20]
Edomae chirashi zushi	Tokyo-style scattered sushi [p133]
Fukin	Cloth used in the kitchen [p18]
Fukusa zushi	Sushi wrapped in a pancake omelette [p158]
Futo maki	Large-roll sushi also known as *date maki* [p192]
Gari	Pickled ginger [p28, 231]
Gomoko zushi	Scattered sushi – "five item sushi" [p138]
Gunkan maki	Nigiri sushi wrapped with nori to hold loose toppings [p218]
Hamachi	Yellowtail tuna [p129]
Hamaguri	Venus clam [p126]
Hangiri	Wooden rice tub [p18]
Hashi	Chopsticks
Hōchō	General term for knives [p20]
Hikari mono	Term for shiny, oily fish [p54, 56]
Hirame	Term for flat fish with eyes on the left side of the head [p76, 78]
Hoso maki	Thin-rolled sushi [p186]
Hotate gai	Scallops [p118, 122]
Ika	Squid [p112]
Ikura	Salmon roe [p125]
Inari zushi	*Abura age* stuffed with sushi rice [p150, 152]
Iri goma	Toasted sesame seeds [p32], can be white or black
Ise ebi	Lobster [p104]
Itamae	The sushi chef [p11]
Iwashi	Sardine [p56]
Kaki	Oysters [p118, 122]
Kampyō	Strips of dried gourd [p24, 30]
Kani	Crab [p98, 128]
Karei	Term for flat fish with eyes on the side of the head [p80, 82]
Katsuo	Bonito [p58]
Katsuo bushi	Dried bonito flakes [p32, 39]
Kazunoko	Herring roes [p56, 125]
Kodomo zushi	Children's sushi [p182]
Kome	Japanese-style rice [p26]
Konbu	Kelp, usually dried [p32]
Maguro	Tuna [p60]
Makajiki	Swordfish [p129]

Maki zushi	Rolled sushi, called *nori maki* if made with nori seaweed [p184]
Makisu	Mat made of bamboo strips for making roll sushi [p23, 184]
Matsukawa zukuri	"Pine bark method" of tenderizing fish skin [p94]
Matō dai	John Dory [p66]
Mirin	Sweet rice wine for cooking [p29]
Miru gai	Horse clam [p127]
Miso shiru	Soup made with soy bean paste [p235, 238]
Nigiri zushi	Sushi rice with fish, vegetables, or omelette
Nishin	Herring [p56]
Nori	Dark seaweed pressed into thin sheets [p26]
Oho toro	Fattiest cut of tuna [p61]
Ohyō garei	Halibut [p82]
Omakase	Chef's choice
Oshi zushi	Pressed sushi [p168]
Oshibako	Pressed sushi mold [p23, 168]
Oshibori	Moistened heated towel
Oshi zushi	Pressed sushi [p168]
Renkon	Lotus roots [p33]
Saba	Mackerel [p62]
Sai bashi	Cooking chopsticks [p19]
Sake	Rice wine [p29, 233] – the same word is used for salmon [p64]
Sanmai oroshi	Three-piece filleting technique for round fish [p72]
Sashimi	Sliced or prepared raw fish [p240]
Sayori	Garfish [p127]
Shamoji	Flat rice-serving spoon [p18]
Shako	Mantis shrimp [p127]
Shari	Term for sushi rice
Shime saba	Vinegar-marinated mackerel [p92]
Shiitake	Type of Japanese mushroom [p31]
Shiso	Japanese mint, perilla [p31]
Shita birame	Dover sole [p129]

Shōyu	Japanese soy sauce [p28, 230]
Soboro	Ground fish, usually pink [p47]
Su	Rice vinegar [p29]
Sui mono	Clear soup [p235, 236]
Sushi meshi	Prepared rice for sushi [p34]
Suzuki	Sea bass [p68]
Tai [also Ma dai]	Japanese red snapper [p70, 94]
Tako	Octopus [p112]
Tamago soboro	Scrambled eggs [p43]
Tamari	Wheat-free soy sauce [p28]
Tataki	Cooking method – rapid searing then cooling of the meat [p146]
Temaki zushi	Hand-rolled sushi [p204]
Temari zushi	Sushi balls [p222]
Teriyaki sauce	Thicker, sweetened soy sauce [p164]
Tobiko	Flying fish roe [p124]
Tofu	Soybean curd [p238]
Toro	Cut of tuna – see *chu toro, oho toro*
Tsuma / kazari	Garnishes / decorations [p48]
Unagi	Freshwater eel [p128]
Uni	Sea urchin [p124]
Uramaki	Inside-out rolled sushi [p196]
Usuba bōchō	Vegetable knife [p20]
Usuyaki tamago	Thin, pancake omelette [p44]
Wakita	"Side cutting board" or assistant sushi chef [p11]
Wasabi	Green, hot Japanese type of horseradish [p27]
Yanagi bōchō	Vegetable knife [p20]
Zaru	Bamboo strainer [p19]
Zāsai	Chinese pickled vegetable [p180]

Notable restaurants directory sushi bars

Australia

MELBOURNE

Mizu
133 Commercial Road,
South Yarra
Tel: 9827 1141

Misuzu's
7 Victoria Avenue,
Albert Park
Tel: 9699 9022

**Japonica Japanese
Restaurant**
Shop 6/180 Toorak Road,
South Yarra
Tel: 9827 2968

Sozai
1221 High Street,
Malvern
Tel: 9824 8200

Yuu
137 Flinders Lane,
Melbourne
Tel: 9639 7073

**Kanpai Japanese
Restaurant**
569 Chapel Street,
South Yarra
Tel: 9827 4379

**Kazen
Japanese Cafe**
201 Brunswick Street,
Fitzroy
Tel: 9417 3270

Akari 177
177 Brunswick Street,
Fitzroy
Tel: 9419 3786

**Aya Japanese
Restaurant**
1193 High Street,
Armadale
Tel: 9822 9571

**Hibari Japanese
Restaurant**
479 Malvern Road,
South Yarra
Tel: 9827 0155

SYDNEY

**Ju Ju's Japanese
Restaurant**
Shop 320, Kingsgate
Shopping Centre,
Kings Cross
Tel: 9357 7100

**Asakusa Japanese
Restaurant**
119 King Street,
Newtown
Tel: 9519 8530

Sushi Suma
421 Cleveland Street,
Surry Hills
Tel: 9698 8873

BRISBANE

Domo
Shop 1,
421 Brunswick Street,
Fortitude Valley
Tel: 3252 2588

Kabuki
The Stamford Plaza,
Edward Street
(cnr Margaret Street),
Brisbane
Tel: 3221 1999

Oshin
256 Adelaide Street,
Brisbane,
Tel: 3229 0410

Canada

VANCOUVER

Tojo's Restaurant
202–777 Broadway Street,
Vancouver,
BC V5Z 4J7
Tel: 604-872-8050
www.tojos.com

**Shijo Japanese
Restaurant**
1926 4th Avenue,
Vancouver,
BC V6J 1M5
Tel: 604-732-4876

Zen Japanese Restaurant
2232 Marine Drive,
West Vancouver,
BC V7V 1K4
Tel: 604-925-0667

TORONTO

Hiro Sushi
171 King Street East,
Toronto,
ON M5A 1J4
Tel: 416-304-0550

Tempo
596 College Street,
Toronto, ON M6G 1B4
Tel: 416-531-2822

Nami
55 Adelaide Street East,
Toronto, ON M5C 1K6
Tel: 416-362-7373

OTTAWA

Kinki
41 York Street,
Ottawa, ON K1N 5S7
Tel: 613-789-9559

Suisha Gardens
208 Slater Street,
Ottawa,
ON K1P 5H8
Tel: 613-236-9602

MONTREAL

Mikado
368 Laurier West,
Montreal,
QC H2V 2K7
Tel: 514-279-4809

Soto
3527 St. Laurent,
Montreal,
QC H2X 2T6
Tel: 514-842-1150
www.restaurantsoto.com

United Kingdom

LONDON

Café Japan
626 Finchley Road,
London, NW11 7RR
Tel: (020) 8455 6854

Defune
34 George Street,
London, W1U 7DP
Tel: (020) 7935 8311

Matsuri
15 Bury Street,
London, SW1Y 6AL
Tel: (020) 7930 7010

Sushi Hiro
1 Station Parade,
Ealing Common,
London, W5 3LD
Tel: (020) 8896 3175

Yoshino
3 Piccadilly Place,
London, W1V 9PD
Tel: (020) 7287 6622

Zuma
5 Raphael Street,
London, SW7 1DR
Tel: (020) 7584 1010

OUTSIDE LONDON

Azuma
4 Byron Place,
Triangle South,
Bristol, BS8 1JT
Tel: (0117) 927 6864

Chikako's
10–11 Mill Lane,
Cardiff, CF1 1FL
Tel: (029) 2066 5279

Daruma-ya
Unit 5, Commercial Quay,
82 Commercial Street,
Edinburgh, EH6 6LX
Tel: (0131) 554 7660

Fumi
248 Durham Road,
Gateshead, NE8 4JR
Tel: (0191) 477 1152

Fusion
41 Byres Road,
Glasgow, G11 5RG
Tel: (0141) 339 3666

Notsushi
Imperial Court,
Exchange Street East,
Liverpool, L2 3PH
(0151) 236 0643

Sapporo Teppanyaki
38–40 Preston Street,
Brighton, BN1 2HP
Tel: (01273) 777 880

United States

ATLANTA, GA

Nakato
1776 Cheshire Bridge Rd,
NE Atlanta, GA,
30324-4922
Tel: (404) 873-6582

BOSTON, MA

Ginza
19 Hudson Street,
Boston, MA, 02111-1902
Tel: (617) 383-2261

Fugakyu
1280 Beacon Street,
Brookline, MA,
02446-3718
Tel: (617) 734-1268

CHICAGO, IL

Kamehachi
1400 N Wells,
Chicago, IL, 60610
Tel: (312) 664-3663

Sushido
1443 W Fullerton Avenue,
Chicago, IL, 60614
Tel: (773) 472-9066

DENVER, CO

Japon
1028 South Gaylord Street,
Denver, CO, 80209
Tel: (303) 744-0330

FLORIDA

Sushi Rock Café
1351 Collins Avenue,
Miami Beach, FL,
33139-4259
Tel: (305) 532-2133

HONOLULU, HI

Kyo-Ya
2057 Kalakaua Avenue,
Honolulu, HI, 96815-2044
Tel: (808) 947-3911

LOS ANGELES, CA

Sushi Nozawa
11288 Ventura Boulevard,
Suite C, Studio City,
CA, 91604-3149
Tel: (818) 508-7017

Nobu
3835 Cross Creek Road,
Malibu, CA, 90265
Tel: (310) 317-9140

NEW ORLEANS, LA

Ninja Restaurant
8433 Oak Street,
New Orleans, LA, 70118
Tel: (504) 866-1119

NEW YORK, NY

Honmura An
170 Mercer Street,
New York, NY,
10012-3244
Tel: (212) 334-5253

Nobu
105 Hudson Street,
New York, NY,
10013-0500
Tel: (212) 219-0500

Tomoe Sushi
172 Thompson Street,
New York, NY,
10012-2576
Tel: (212) 777-9346

NEW JERSEY

Nikko
881 Route 10 E,
Whippany, NJ,
07981-1104
Tel: (973) 428-0787

PHILADELPHIA, PA

Hikaru Restaurant
4348 Main Street,
Philadelphia, PA,
19127-1438
Tel: (215) 487-3500

PHOENIX, AZ

**Ra Sushi Bar and
Restaurant**
3815 N Scottsdale Road,
Scottsdale, AZ, 85251
Tel: (480) 990-9256
www.rasushi.com

SAN FRANCISCO, CA

Kabuto Sushi
5116 Geary Boulevard,
San Francisco, CA, 94118
Tel: (415) 752-5652

Tokyo Go Go
3174 16th Street,
San Francisco, CA, 94110
Tel: (415) 864-2288

SEATTLE, WA

I Love Sushi
1001 Fairview Avenue N,
Seattle, WA, 98109
Tel: (206) 625-9604

Shiro's
2401 2nd Avenue,
Seattle, WA, 98121
Tel: (206) 443-9844

TEXAS

**Nara Restaurant
& Sushi Bar**
11124 Westheimer,
Houston, TX,
77042-3291
Tel: (713) 266-2255

WASHINGTON, DC

Makoto
4822 MacArthur
Boulevard NW,
Washington, DC,
20007-1557
Tel: (202) 298-6866

Kaz Sushi Bistro
1915 I Street NW,
Washington, DC,
20006-2107
Tel: (202) 530-5500

Japanese retailers and fish suppliers

Most of the ingredients mentioned in this book are readily available in good supermarkets. If your supermarket doesn't stock a certain item and there is no specialty Japanese store nearby, you can usually order the specific product over the internet. It can sometimes be difficult to find a good fishseller or store, but when you do, hold onto them. Be sure to tell them that you are going to use the fish for sushi.

Australia

Anegawa Supermarket
Specialist Asian supplier
7/17 Waters Road,
Neutral Bay, Sydney
Tel: 9904 4177

Asian Foods Ltd
Specialist Asian supplier
101–105 Grafton Street,
Cairns QLD 4870
Tel: 4052 1510

Burlington Supermarket
Asian supplier
TC Beirne Centre Shop 27,
Chinatown Mall,
Brisbane 4000
Tel: 3216 0828

Claringbold's Seafood
Seafood supplier
Prahran Market,
Commercial Road,
Prahran, Melbourne
Tel: 9826 8381

Fisch Shop
Seafood and sushi supplies
251A Chadstone
Shopping Centre,
Chadstone 3148
Tel: 9568 1138

Mackay Reef Fish Supplies
Fresh fish supplier
2 River Street,
Mackay 4740
Tel: 4957 6497

Randwick Oriental Supermarket
Specialist Asian supplier
61 Belmore Road,
Randwick, Sydney
Tel: 9398 2192

Sushi Sushi
Sushi supplies
Chadstone Shopping
Centre, Chadstone
Tel: 9568 3882

Sydney Fish Market
*Many suppliers of
excellent fresh fish*
cnr of Pyrmont Bridge Road
and Bank St, Pyrmont,
NSW 2009
Tel: 9660 0866

Tokyo Mart
Specialist Asian supplier
Shop 27, Northbridge
Plaza, Cnr of Eastern Valley
Way and Sailors Bay Road,
Northbridge, Sydney
Tel: 9958 6860

www.seafoodshop.com.au
*Online seafood
supplier*
Seafood shop,
PO Box 1167,
Stafford City,
QLD 4053
Tel: 3355 4333

Canada

Fujiya
*Fish and Japanese
foods retailer*
912 Clark Drive,
Vancouver,
BC V5L 3J8
Tel: 604-251-3711

Fujiya
*Fish and Japanese
foods retailer*
Suite 112,
1050 W. Pender Street,
Vancouver BC
Tel: 604-608-1050

Lapointe Fish
Online fish supplies
445 Catherine Street,
Ottawa,
Ontario K1R 5T7
Tel: 613-233-6221

Pacific Coast Wasabi Ltd.
Fresh wasabi growers
450–1050 Alberni Street,
Vancouver BC, V6E 1A3
www.wasabia.ca

Pure Food Fish Market
Fresh fish supplier
Pike Place Market,
Seattle WA
Tel: 206-622-5765
www.freshseafood.com

Sanko
Japanese groceries
730 Queen Street West,
Toronto, ON M6J 1E8
Tel: 416-703-4550
www.toronto-sanko.com

United Kingdom

Akaneya
Japanese food store
81 Northumberland Ave.,
Reading, RG2 7PT
Tel: (0118) 931 0448

Arigato
Japanese supermarket
48-50 Brewer Street,
London, W1F 9TG
Tel: (020) 7287 1722

Atari-ya
Fish and Japanese foods
Monkville Parade,
Finchley Road, London,
NW11 0AL
Tel: (020) 8458 7626

Atari-ya
Fish and Japanese foods
West Acton Branch,
7 Station Parade,
Noel Road,
London, W3 0DS
Tel: (020) 8896 1552

Chalmers & Gray
Fresh and smoked fish
67 Notting Hill Gate,
London,
W11 3JS
Tel: (020) 7221 6177

Miura Foods
Japanese food suppliers
44 Coombe Road,
Norbiton,
Nr Kingston,
Surrey, KT2 7AE

Miura Foods
Japanese food suppliers
5 Limpsfield Road,
Sanderstead,
Surrey, CR2 9LA
Tel: (020) 8651 4498

Intel Supermarket
Japanese food suppliers
126 Malden Road,
New Malden,
Surrey, KT3 6DD
Tel: (020) 8942 9552

Jasmin
c/o Stanton House Hotel
Japanese food suppliers
The Avenue,
Station Fitzwarren,
Swindon, Wiltshire,
SN6 7SE
(Wed, Fri, Sun 3–6pm)
Tel: (01793) 861777

Midori c/o
Anglo-Japan Services Ltd
Japanese food suppliers
19 Marlborough Place,
Brighton,
East Sussex, BN1 1UB
Tel: (01273) 601460

Mount Fuji International
Japanese food online
Shrewsbury, SY4 1AS
Tel: (01743) 741169
www.mountfuji.co.uk

Oriental City
Japanese food suppliers
399 Edgeware Road,
Colindale,
London, NW9 0JJ
Tel: (020) 8200 0009

Setsu Japanese Food
Japanese food suppliers
196a Heaton Road,
Newcastle Upon Tyne,
NE6 5HP
Tel: (0191) 265 9970

Steve Hatt Fishmongers
Fresh and smoked fish
88–90 Essex Road,
London, N1 8LU
Tel: (020) 7226 3963

T K Trading
Japanese food supplies
Unit 6/76,
The Chase Centre,
8 Chase Road,
North Acton,
London, NW10 6QD
Tel: (020) 8453 1001

United States

99 Ranch/Tawa Market
Japanese food market
7330 Clairemont
Mesa Blvd.,
San Diego, CA 92111
Tel: (858) 974-8899

99 Ranch/Tawa Market
for other outlets see:
www.99ranch.com

The CMC Company
Online exotic food outlet
P.O. Drawer 322 Avalon,
NJ 08202
Tel: 1-800-262-2780
www.thecmccompany.com

Katagiri
Large Japanese market
224 East 59th Street,
New York,
NY 10022
Tel: (212) 755-3566
www.katagiri.com

**Maine Coast Sea
Vegetables**
Specialty seaweed supplier
3 Georges Pond Road,
Franklin, ME 04634
Tel: (207) 565-2907
www.seaveg.com

Mistuwa Market
Japanese food market
333 S. Alameda Street,
Los Angeles,
CA 90013
Tel: (213) 687-6699

Mistuwa Market
Japanese food market
675 Saratoga Avenue,
San Jose, CA 95129
Tel: (408) 255-6699

Mistuwa Market
Japanese food market
100 E. Algonquin Road,
Arlington Heights,
IL 60005
Tel: (847) 956-6699

Mistuwa Market
Japanese food market
595 River Road,
Edgewater, NJ 07020
Tel: (201) 941-9113

Mistuwa Market
for other outlets see:
www.mitsuwa.com

Ohana Seafood Market
Fresh fish supplier
168 Lake Street South,
Kirkland,
WA 98033
Tel: 1-800-347-4754
www.fish2go.com

Pacific Farms USA LP
Fresh wasabi supplier
88420 Highway 101 N,
Florence, OR 97430
Tel: (800) 927-2248
www.freshwasabi.com

www.asiafoods.com
Online Asian food supplier
Mailing address:
AsiaFoods.com
18-20 Oxford Street,
Boston,
MA 02111
Tel: 1-877-902-0841

www.quickspice.com
Asian food supplier
Tel: (800) 553-5008

Sushi Foods Company
*Online supplier of sushi
supplies and utensils*
San Diego, California
Tel: 1-888-81-78744
Tel: 1-619-222-3732
www.sushifoods.com

Uwajimaya
*Japanese food and
equipment*
600 5th Avenue South,
#100, Seattle, WA 98104
Tel: (206) 624-6248

Index

Acknowledgments

Author's Appreciation

I would like to thank Rosie and Eric of Books for Cooks who supported me throughout and without whose help this book would not have started. A big thank you to Ian O'Leary and his French assistant, Ludo, for taking beautiful photographs and providing good music during the long photo shoot. I also would like to thank all the members of the team of Dorling Kindersley but especially Mary-Clare Jerram, Tracy Killick, Sara Robin and Hugh Thompson for their very professional but human support. A huge gratitude goes to Nasim Mawji for her transatlantic editing. My special thank you to Jasper Morris of Morris & Verdin [Wine Merchants] for sharing his wine expertise. Thank you to Kalpana Brijnath, Eve Pleming and Simon May for lending me "hands" for the party photo shoot. But my final and biggest thank you goes to my long-suffering English husband, Stephen, for his unlimited support and Maxi, Frederick and Dominic, my three sons for being tireless guinea pigs.

Dorling Kindersley would like to thank Jenny Jones for her editorial work at the beginning and Rosie Hopper for her inspirational work as a stylist.
Picture credits: Peter Wilson 6bl, 8tl.

For supplying china:

Ceramica Blue www.ceramicablue.co.uk

New Wave Tableware supplied by Villeroy and Boch Tel: (020) 8871 0011

The Conran Shop Ltd., Michelin House, 81 Fulham Road, London SW3 6RD
Tel: (020) 7589 7401 www.conran.com

NOM, 7–9 Exhibition Road, South Kensington, London, SW7 6RD
Tel: (020) 7590 0890

Handmade boat dishes by Sarah Vernon www.studiopottery.co.uk

Thanks to Jasper Morris for his expertise and donating all the wines for the photo shoot.
Mr. Jasper Morris of Morris & Verdin
Unit 2, Bankside Industrial Estate, Sumner Street, London SE1 9JZ
Tel: (020) 7921 5300

Finally many thanks to Valerie Chandler for the index.